Mom, Interrupted

The story of the sole survivor of one of
South Africa's most brutal family murders

Debbie Adlington
as told to
Gerda Kruger

ZEBRA

Published by Zebra Press
an imprint of Struik Publishers
(a division of New Holland Publishing (South Africa) (Pty) Ltd)
PO Box 1144, Cape Town, 8000
New Holland Publishing is a member of Johnnic Communications Ltd

www.zebrapress.co.za

First published 2006

1 3 5 7 9 10 8 6 4 2

Publication © Zebra Press 2006
Text © Gerda Kruger 2006

Cover photographs: © *Cape Argus*/Trace Images (main photo); © Roy Wigley/*Cape Argus*/Trace Images (middle left); © Debbie Adlington (top and bottom left)

All rights reserved. No part of this publication may be reproduced, stored in a retrieval system or transmitted, in any form or by any means, electronic, mechanical, photocopying, recording or otherwise, without the prior written permission of the copyright owners.

PUBLISHING MANAGER:	Marlene Fryer
MANAGING EDITOR:	Robert Plummer
EDITOR:	Marléne Burger
PROOFREADER:	Ronel Richter-Herbert
COVER AND TEXT DESIGNER:	Natascha Adendorff-Olivier
TYPESETTER:	Monique van den Berg
PHOTO RESEARCHER:	Colette Stott
PRODUCTION MANAGER:	Valerie Kömmer

Set in 11.5 pt on 17 pt Adobe Caslon

Reproduction by Hirt & Carter (Cape) (Pty) Ltd
Printed and bound by Paarl Print, Oosterland Street, Paarl, South Africa

ISBN 1 77022 003 8

IMAGES OF AFRICA
PHOTO LIBRARY

Over 40 000 unique African images available to purchase
from our image bank at www.imagesofafrica.co.za

GERDA KRUGER is a part-time writer and former journalist with many years of writing experience. She is currently the executive director responsible for Communication and Marketing at the University of Cape Town. She recently won a national competition for creative writing, and her winning story was published in *Nobody ever said Aids – Stories and poems from Southern Africa*. *Mom, Interrupted* is her first book.

*Dedicated to Debbie's children:
Kevin, Katelyn and Craig,
and their new sister, Kylie-Ann*

Contents

ACKNOWLEDGEMENTS ix
WRITER'S NOTE xiii

1 The calling 1
2 Tony 9
3 My children 25
4 Hazel 39
5 Decisions made, lessons learned 47
6 Life changes 59
7 The last twenty-four hours 71
8 Code Red 83
9 Survival 97
10 Awakenings 101
11 Finding my feet 115
12 Starting over 125
13 Homeward bound 137
14 A new beginning 145
15 Alone no more 159

REFLECTIONS 165

Acknowledgements

THERE ARE SO MANY PEOPLE WHO SUPPORTED ME in my time of most urgent need.

In the first instance, I am eternally grateful to the emergency personnel who kept me safe and stabilised until specialists could ensure my life was saved. My thanks also to the medical and other professional staff – surgeons, nurses, physiotherapists, cleaners, trauma counsellors and psychologists – who all played a meaningful role in my recovery.

My parents, brothers and extended family formed the emotional and physical support base I needed and that allowed me to rise from the depths of trauma. There were many moments when life seemed unimportant and utterly intolerable. At those times, my closest family members were there – quietly and consistently. I can never repay the love that I felt emanating from them. The only thing I can do is love them equally in return. That is my promise.

So many friends spent hours making conversation during a time when I was not even listening, let alone responding to them. They came to my bedside, again and again, leaving their own families for an hour or two in order to provide me with a sense that I was not alone.

In the days after the event, I often felt utterly lonely and unsure about how and why I should continue living. But my friends, each in his or her own way, insisted that I remain connected to them and, slowly but surely, this gave me a bridge to cross from that cold, painful place to a new home. It is not possible to name all my 'bridge builders' in this book, but I hold them all in my heart. Their faces remain my memory of the most selfless caring. I am deeply indebted to them all.

To Gerda Kruger, I owe great and special thanks. For nearly two years we spent hours and hours together going through all the details of my life. Many moments were funny, while others were extremely hard to share. Gerda made the process easy and safe. In the end, it felt as though she knew more about me than I did myself. There were so many cups of coffee at Savannah on Saturday mornings and many, many words spoken. I don't really know how it all came together in the end, but it did, and for that I have Gerda to thank.

As we were writing this book, I was aware that many people who knew Tony might have their own views on why he did what he did. This book reflects my own view. It is the tale of my life as I experienced it. I fully accept that other people might see matters differently. I also know that looking in from the outside can never be the same as living in or through a particular set of circumstances. It is inevitable that my story reflects *my* sense of what occurred and that this may differ from the experience or memories of others, even if they were involved in the same events.

I have not attempted to find a final answer for all that happened. Nor have I even tried to understand the reasons for family murders. These events and the underlying causes are deeply complicated. I have not attempted to unravel this phenomenon here, merely to tell my story as I lived and felt it. For me, that has been an important part of my healing.

Acknowledgements

Lastly, thank you to those who will read this book and to the many anonymous people who were touched by what had happened to me. So many people showed so much compassion on hearing about the destruction of my immediate family; so many others expressed deep empathy, although they did not know me. I was astounded by my fellow human beings.

There were those who supported the Debbie Adlington Appeal Fund and in this way helped, among other things, to pay my many medical bills.

There were those who sent a message, a prayer, a good thought. I found kindness in the aisles of supermarkets and in shopping malls, over counters at the bank, via radio talk shows. I was deeply touched by all these expressions of support. This book is a way of thanking those whose names, in many cases, I might never know, but to whom I owe a great debt of gratitude.

I hope that this book will have some meaning for others. It has already helped my healing process, but my fervent wish is that it will also assist someone else – that somewhere, someone will recognise a situation or understand their own situation better and perhaps be able to change it. If just one sentence strikes a chord somewhere and brings relief, assistance, healing or comfort, it will all have been worthwhile.

My own trauma destroyed all trust in people and in life. I have since regained my faith in both. How could I not, when I was shown so much kindness and love? Each one who reached out to me, helped in some way to make me whole again. Thank you.

DEBBIE ADLINGTON

Writer's note

WRITING THIS BOOK WAS TRULY A BLESSING. IN one way, it was easy. Debbie had reflected on aspects of her life so much that she was wonderfully clear on what events took place, how she felt and what the impact on her had been.

On the other hand, it was hard to hear a story filled with so much pain and longing. I was left with a profound sadness for the lives that were lost and with sincere admiration for the courage shown by the woman who remained behind – alone.

It would be impossible to fully reflect on the pages that follow the enormity of the pain that Debbie must have felt immediately after the murders and in coming to terms with what had happened. My hope, however, is that I have succeeded in capturing her undeniable bravery and extraordinary spirit.

I am grateful to Debbie and everyone else who gave up so many hours for so many interviews. My thanks also to Marlene Fryer at Zebra Press and to Marléne Burger for the considerate editing of the book.

My intention was not merely to write about a tragedy, but rather to focus on how the sole survivor dealt with her massive trauma and attempted to make sense of it.

My hope is that Debbie's story will heighten awareness on the issue of famicide and that it will bring comfort to those who might be struggling to come to grips with fear and trauma, regardless of the cause.

GERDA KRUGER

I

The calling

MY SON IS SCREAMING. I CAN HEAR HIM CALLING me: *Mommy! Mommy!* The sound is crystal clear, immediate, and there is a tone of urgency that jolts my entire being. Kevin is my eldest son. He is crying out. He needs me!

Kevin? Kevin? Are my lips forming his name in response, or am I only picturing the letters of his name in my mind? I can't be sure … Here, Kevin! Mommy's here! Something doesn't feel right. Instinctively I look around, trying to locate him. I don't know where he is! It's as though he is invisible. Frantic now, I try again, but it's as though he's hidden in some place that disturbs me just to think about. Then it's quiet, and I retreat into a dream-like place.

Suddenly, I sit up with a jerk. I shudder as I hear the calling again, distinct, desperate now. *Mommy! Mommy!*

Again I respond, so certain that he is close by, perhaps even in the same room. The urge to find him immediately is irresistible. My body jerks again, I look around. This room is unfamiliar. If only I wasn't so confused! Where am I? Where is Kevin? I call his name again. Kevin? Where are you, honey?

There is no reply, and my frustration becomes intolerable. Something is holding me back. There is an indescribable resistance. My mind is hazy, but I feel a powerful sense of loss. Is Kevin lost? Am I? Why can't I help my son?

There are people all around me. I don't recognise their faces or anything about the room. It infuriates me to see them staring at me, curiously fixated, their eyes filled with concern. But they remain oddly removed from me. A terrible fear takes hold of me and I scream, insisting that they must find Kevin.

'Where is Kevin? Can't you hear him calling? Find him, bring him to me! Bring him to me now!'

I plunge into a sea of nauseating emotion. Where are the other kids? Something is wrong ... I *know* that, but I can't figure out what the problem is. Is Katelyn also here? What about Craig? He's too little to be left alone. Are they here? Are they all together? Are they with Tony? Is Hazel there to protect them? Will she bark if someone tries to hurt them?

I feel a definite sense of unease, now. Is it fear? Danger? I can't hold onto my thoughts long enough to work it all out. All that lingers, overwhelmingly, is a desperate sense of urgency about my children.

'Bring them to me, please,' I beg. They need to be fed, they have things to do. There's homework to complete. I have to start making supper. We need to get home. Is Tony picking me up? Are the children waiting for me somewhere? Are they here, I ask, again and again, but all I get are silent stares from the strangers who surround me.

Tears run down my cheeks and drip onto my chest. They feel like warm water. I am crying, but I don't know why. What does this all mean? Why can't I understand?

* * *

The calling

In the first days and weeks after the murders of my children and my husband's suicide, as consciousness and life flowed slowly back into my veins, I had no idea what had happened or what lay ahead. My thoughts were jumbled, disconnected wisps and words that had no power to help me make sense of the torturous puzzle that had become my life. Awareness came trickling back in tiny doses. It took days for me to wake up. It took weeks to absorb the reality of my husband's actions on a balmy summer morning just three weeks after Christmas. It took months to fully grasp the impact of being the sole survivor of a gruesome family murder.

It will take years to stop myself involuntarily reaching for a toy or a treat on the supermarket shelves that Kevin, Katelyn or Craig would have loved. It will take the rest of my life to stop seeing their faces in a crowded shopping mall or hearing their voices from across an empty room.

Slowly, slowly, I shed the instinctive urge on waking every morning to get up and start moving, because there was so much to do before school. It seemed to be an eternity before I stopped feeling the sharp sense of energy sweep through me just before I spoke to one of the children, reminding them that it was bedtime, chiding them for making a mess, calling them to come and eat, drawing their attention to something funny on TV. With the passing of the years, I have found many answers, but I have also accepted, albeit only lately, that much will forever remain in question.

I have arrived at the point where knowing all the answers is not the most important thing. Dealing with the reality, moving forward, playing out the hand that I was dealt – those have become my priorities and my daily tasks.

I recognise that I am one of the few. Not many people survive a family murder. In fact, this very seldom happens. In an attempt to understand what happened to my family and why, I have tried to learn as much as possible about the theories and research on the subject, but that doesn't qualify me to shed more light on the phenomenon or confirm any of the expert findings. All I can do is tell my story, for whatever it may be worth to others.

I will never fully understand what took place as the sun rose over the Cape that morning, or why I did not die as well. I will never know if my children called out to me for help as their father carried their mortally wounded bodies through what had been our home. I will always wonder if one of them was conscious and realised that our entire family was being butchered. Did they strain for breath when smoke filled their lungs? Did they see the chaos around them in the study? Did their eyes meet in bewilderment? Did one of them see the others covered in blood? Was their last vision that of Tony putting a gun to his head?

I won't ever know if Kevin's cries for me were real or not. It might be that his calls came from another place, somewhere beyond this earthly plain, to rouse me from the coma I had been in for so long. Perhaps it was his voice that blew life into me again, or perhaps I heard it only in my imagination.

Much of my memory, knowledge and insight about Wednesday 16 January 2002 were gathered gradually, pieced together from official records, the recollections of friends

The calling

and family, newspaper headlines and reports. The rest was found by thinking endlessly – not only about the events of that morning or the night before, but about my entire sixteen-year relationship with Tony, fourteen of them as husband and wife, twelve as parents of three wonderful, loving children – by spending many hours with counsellors and by shedding a small river of tears.

For the longest time while dealing with the fact that the man I loved had taken not only his own life but also the lives of our sons and daughter after brutally attacking me, fear, uncertainty, anxiety and confusion became my closest and constant companions. Many a time I was consumed by anger that bordered on hatred and would rage against Tony, helpless and frustrated that he was not there to see and hear me. There were moments when I hated him so much that I could picture him coming through the door and banging my fists against his chest, but such images never brought relief. It took a long time to bring my anger under control, and even now there are days when I feel it again.

My dreams – nightmares, really – were filled with images of Tony bludgeoning the children with an axe as they lay in their beds, carrying them to the study one by one, dousing them with petrol and setting them alight before pulling the trigger that would obliterate his vision of this ghastly deed and spare him the sight of flames licking at the broken bodies of the three children that had sprung from his loins.

I came to know each of these mental pictures with vivid and heartbreaking intimacy before they finally began to fade and make way for equally gut-wrenching but less harrowing images of my children when they were alive and happy. It was at this point, I think, that I first began to make some sense out of the senseless, but it would still be many months before I was able to rekindle some old friendships and form a few new ones.

At some level, I have stopped looking for my children, but I will never stop longing for them, and I have learned that I don't have to. They are as much a part of me now as they were during the nine months that I carried each of them in my womb, and they will remain so until my dying breath. Their physical presence has been removed, but they live in my heart as surely as the bright African sun will shine tomorrow, and the next day, and for all the days after that. Kevin, Katelyn and Craig, my most precious gifts from God, will always be my children, and I will love them forever.

But there was a time, in the aftermath of my family's destruction, when nothing and no one could have convinced me that I would find love and happiness again, or that my life would come to have meaning once more. I had to stumble through hell first, but what awaited me when I eventually emerged from my dark and desolate pit of loss and sorrow was a new beginning in the most wondrous sense of the term.

While I lay in my hospital bed or spent hours in physical therapy and emotional counselling, it would never have occurred to me that I could choose not to walk my future path alone. It was inconceivable that I would ever again know the joy of nurturing and caring for another human being, or experience anew the wonder of loving and being loved in return. But shortly before the fourth anniversary of the tragedy that had ripped my

The calling

life apart, I gave birth to another child, a little girl whose very existence depends on me, whose future is inextricably entwined with my own.

Only time will tell our mutual fates, but as our life together unfolds, I will take all that I have learned from the past and use it well to protect my fourth child and ensure that the path she follows is a safe and happy one. I know that I won't stop questioning what answers I have found, but since they are *my* answers, they are surely mine to interrogate again and again, over and over. I will continue to wonder, to explore and to learn, and I will endeavour to overcome the horrors that still haunt me; but, above all, I am determined to build a new and peaceful life, filled with goodness and abundant love, for my daughter and myself.

2

Tony

WHEN I MET THE MAN WHO WOULD BECOME THE father of my three children, I was twenty-three years old and somewhat naive. His name was Anthony John Adlington, but everyone called him Tony.

I was working for a group of pharmacies in Durban, where I was born. Tony, nine years older than me, had a small apartment near my workplace and had, in fact, been to the pharmacy, though I had not noticed him at the time. He told me later that he had witnessed me dealing with the complaints of a particularly difficult customer and been impressed by the calm manner in which I handled her extremely rude tirade.

Not long after this incident, I was offered a job at a different pharmacy and, eager for a change of scenery, accepted. This meant that I would no longer be working in the area where Tony lived, and the move might have set me on an entirely different path, but fate dictated otherwise. While we were still merchandising and preparing the shop before opening the doors to customers, my new employer, Dave Stainton, asked me to go to a nearby shopping mall to buy some coffee mugs. In the frenzy of stocking shelves and displaying our wares, we had quite forgotten that we needed them.

Dressed in my pharmacy uniform and with my name clearly visible on a tag pinned to my chest, I prowled the aisles at

Checkers in search of mugs. I was really excited about the new shop and being part of something from the beginning. I was determined to be so good at my job that I would become quite indispensable.

Tony was working for Butterworth Productions, a manufacturer of medical equipment, at the time. As it happened, he left work early that day and went to the supermarket to buy groceries. He ended up in the aisle where I was examining the mugs on offer and asked politely if I knew where he could find the records and tapes. It was 23 November 1985, and compact discs were yet to make their debut.

I was taken aback by his question and wondered why he assumed I would be able to help. As I told him that I didn't work at Checkers and had no idea where he might find what he wanted, I noticed that he was looking at my name. Then I picked up the blue mugs I had chosen and went to pay for them, without giving the strange man another thought.

For the second time in a relatively short period, fate or some other mysterious force had engineered a chance encounter between us, though neither made any real impression on me, and again, that might have been the last time that our paths crossed. Later that afternoon, however, the phone in the pharmacy rang. Dave answered, then passed the receiver to me, joking: 'I can't believe someone's tracked you down already!'

I expected the caller to be a friend or, more likely, one of my old customers, but it was an unfamiliar voice that said politely: 'Hi there. This is Tony. I'm not sure if you remember me. I asked you about tapes and records at Checkers earlier.'

I recalled the tall, lean man, neatly dressed in a suit, who

Tony

had interrupted my mug expedition. Tony told me that he'd seen me before, at the old pharmacy, then asked if I'd like to have supper with him on Friday night. I was young and single and so was he. I hesitated for only a moment before accepting.

As soon as I replaced the receiver, however, I panicked. 'What now?' Dave asked.

'I have to cancel this date,' I replied. 'I've just said yes to a man I've never actually met. I don't know this guy at all!'

Dave, as always, offered sensible advice. 'It'll be fine. Go somewhere decent, somewhere busy. Be sure to take money with you. If you need to call a taxi or a friend, do so immediately. Come on, it will be fine.'

I did as he suggested. We chose a small but popular restaurant close enough to the ocean for a light sea breeze to drift through the open window and play across my shoulders on the hot and humid November night. I had money in my purse but, as it turned out, no need to use it. The food was delicious, the atmosphere romantic and the man seated opposite me, a perfect gentleman.

As we chatted easily about ourselves, our parents, jobs and previous relationships, I studied my self-confident and interesting companion. His face was pleasant and open, his neatly trimmed moustache emphasised a beautiful mouth and perfect white teeth. He had a lovely skin, and his light-brown hair was neatly cut. Contact lenses added a hint of green to his brown eyes. Little did I know, that night, how many times in the future we would be on our knees, shoulder to shoulder, on the floor of bedrooms and bathrooms, searching for one of those tiny plastic discs!

I was attracted to Tony from the start, and over the years

many of my friends remarked on how good-looking he was. His hair gradually thinned out a bit on top and he took to shaving it with clippers, but the broad smile and handsome features became even more appealing as he grew older.

On that first date, we laughed a lot, about silly, unimportant things, as potential young lovers do. It would be a long time before I realised that, even then, Tony was holding something back, keeping some part of himself hidden.

We started seeing one another regularly, and he was great fun to be with. As was my nature, I let myself be led by him; I questioned little and happily went along with the flow of events. We spent much of our time together in his flat, watching television or rented videos. Some evenings we would read or Tony would cook a meal. Neither of us drank much, and Tony was a hard worker who took his job seriously. Many an hour was spent talking about his job, the best way to solve the professional challenges he faced and what path his career might follow.

Soon it was Christmas, and Tony left to visit his parents in Zimbabwe. His father, John, was a medical practitioner in Harare who had been granted custody of two daughters – Shelagh and Penny – from a previous marriage. A few years after his second wife, Ann, gave birth to Tony, they also had a daughter, Jane.

The three sisters adored the only boy in the family, and by all accounts, Tony had a loving relationship with his parents and siblings, as well as a normal, happy childhood. By the time he completed his studies in accountancy, the then Rhodesia was engulfed in civil war. Like all white men of his generation,

Tony

Tony had to do compulsory military service, and he spent two years with the police, in an administrative post, before moving to South Africa.

After school, Tony shared a flat in Harare with Robbie Finch, who was in the air force at the time. They remained friends, and Robbie always described Tony as having been a bright young man who seemed more mature and responsible than his peers. Other members of their circle looked up to Tony, who was from a well-to-do family, self-assured, serious about his future and always seemed to be in control, no matter what the situation. He was also, according to Robbie, a 'one-woman man', even as a student.

Long after Tony died, however, Robbie and I agreed that there was always a secretive, intensely private side to him that neither of us had known or understood. From the beginning, Robbie said, Tony had set extremely high standards for himself, especially in terms of what he wanted to achieve financially, and never shared any of his problems with his friends.

When Tony went to Harare in December 1985, I stayed in his apartment for two weeks. He had suggested that I would be both safer and more comfortable there than in my own small flat, and he was right. When he called me on Christmas Day, I was surprised to hear him say: 'Why don't you think about giving up your flat and moving in with me permanently?'

I didn't give him an answer immediately, but over the next few days, I thought about nothing else. It seemed a crazy thing to do when we had known one another for only a few weeks, but we were in love, enjoyed one another's company and liked being together. Still, I was scared of making a mistake and needed to be sure that moving in with Tony would not be something I would later regret.

Unable to decide, I did what I had always done when faced with a dilemma: I called my parents. My wonderful father, David, and equally wonderful mother, Margaret, were my safety net. Of course we had our differences from time to time, but they loved me unconditionally and their stable, loving marriage was an example that influenced my thinking on relationships in very definite ways.

My childhood had been a happy one. I was the middle child and only girl. My older brother Nigel was my protector and mentor. Like all siblings, we had more than our fair share of teenage fights, but we cared deeply for each other and had loads of fun.

Bruce, my younger brother, was born when I was eight. For a long time, he was pretty much a 'real live toy', much better than any doll! I can still see him running after me on his little toddler's legs, calling 'Bebbie! Bebbie!' I loved him madly and was over the moon when his cot was placed beside my bed when he was old enough. Some nights, when he woke up crying, I would jump out of bed to put a dummy or bottle back into his mouth. Years later, my mom told me that she always heard Bruce crying, but would listen for a moment or two until he grew quiet. Only then, knowing that I had attended to him, would she go back to sleep.

It is amazing how life turns out. My baby brother grew up to be an experienced and well-respected member of the South African Police Service's serious and violent crimes unit, and a tower of strength when I had to start my life over from scratch.

Tony

When I was five, my parents moved into the house at Amanzimtoti that, even after we had all created our own, independent lives, my brothers and I still called 'home'. It was perched on the edge of a cliff, and from a clump of trees five metres away from the house, a path led down to the beach. As a child, I would wander down the face of the cliff and stroll across the railway line to the golden sands that stretched as far as the eye could see. That beach became our playground, a lovely place where we would picnic with our parents in what I look back on as an absolutely idyllic childhood.

I was a skinny little girl. For most of my life I had waist-length blonde hair, and according to my Mom, I was fiercely independent by the age of two. I wouldn't let anyone hold my hand when crossing a street and wanted to do everything for myself. Both the primary and high school that I attended in Amanzimtoti were within walking distance of the house. My dad drove us to school every morning, but I loved to walk home in the afternoons, though it could be extremely hot in summer.

My days were filled with school, the beach, fun with my brothers and dancing. I loved ballet and modern dancing and spent a lot of time learning both. I had many friends in the neighbourhood and, with crime virtually unheard of in the area, we children came and went to one another's homes unhindered.

Though closer in age to Bruce than to me, Isobel Caitano, who lived across the street, was one of my regular playmates. In time, she would qualify as a specialised intensive-care nurse, marry and move away from Durban, only to re-enter our lives and offer my parents and me help and support in circumstances that we could never have imagined.

Given my happy, largely uncomplicated background, it was only natural that I would seek guidance from my parents while contemplating a permanent move into Tony's flat and thus also his life. My dreams were quite simple. I wanted the kind of relationship that my parents had shared for almost a quarter-century. I wanted a husband to love and children to care for and enjoy as they grew up to become good people.

I was keen to pursue my relationship with Tony, but anxious not to make a mistake. Due to bad judgement on my part, I was living with the reality that my short-lived first marriage had failed, and I wanted to be sure that if I agreed to live with Tony, I would be committing to something stable and permanent.

I had just turned twenty when I met my ex-husband, who, like Tony, was an accountant. What *was* it with me and the bean counters? He was doing his compulsory national military service and had become friendly with my brother. No one in the family was pleased when we started dating, let alone when we got married. It turned out to be what I considered a catastrophe, and I did not want to repeat my mistake. In a typical scenario, I was the last person to find out what my husband was really like. When people hinted that he was seeing other women, I would not believe them, but the marriage was really terrible for both of us. I suspect that he felt trapped, while I was deeply disappointed in what married life appeared to be.

One night he was extremely late getting home from work and a screaming match ensued. It ended with him shoving me against a wall so hard that my lip split and started bleeding. I calmed things down, got out of our flat as soon as I could

Tony

and went to my parents' home. We had been married for one year and ten months and it felt awful to admit that we had made a horrible mistake. After our fight he pleaded with me to stay, and eventually, because I felt at least partly to blame, I agreed. In the next breath, however, he made it clear that I would have to accept that he would do as he pleased. I knew then that things would never work between us, and we divorced soon afterwards.

I was relieved but also sad that it was over. In my little world, marriage was supposed to last forever, and I was the first in our family to fail in this regard. My dreams were shattered, and I certainly did not want a repeat performance with Tony, but how could I know if he was the right man for me? What if he didn't want to get married? What if he got bored after a while and left me? What if I realised at some point that I didn't want to spend the rest of my life with him?

These and other questions tumbled around in my mind for days, but by the time Tony got back from Zimbabwe, I had an answer. I agreed to move in with him, but insisted on keeping my flat, at least for a while. Apart from being an 'insurance policy', this would allow me to keep Billy, a tame cockatiel that I had acquired about a year before.

I'd seen Billy at a pet shop. Because he had a deformed leg, no one wanted to buy him. When the store owner noticed my interest, he said I could have Billy for free, provided I promised to give him a good home. Until I met Tony, the bird was my favourite companion. He had the run of the apartment, following me from place to place while I spoke to him about anything and everything. For the first couple of months that

Mom, Interrupted

Tony and I lived together, I would spend a little time at my flat every evening to feed, touch and talk to Billy. Once I felt more secure with Tony, I gave up my flat and Billy came to live with us.

He seemed pleased with his new home, but Tony was concerned about the bird soiling the apartment, so Billy spent the days in his cage, which he neither liked nor was used to. By the time I got home in the evenings, he was squawking loudly and I would let him out immediately. I thought Tony would relent after a while, but he never really took to Billy, and after a few weeks I realised that Billy was unhappy. My mom agreed to take him, but soon afterwards he flew away. Luckily, an elderly woman found him on her balcony and contacted my mother in response to an advertisement she had placed in the newspaper, but it wasn't long before Billy took flight again. We never found him.

In hindsight, perhaps I should have flown away as well. I do know that the cockatiel was the first sacrifice I made to please Tony, but, at the time, even though I loved that bird, I didn't fight to keep him. We never discussed Billy again, but I came to understand, much later, that the way we had dealt with the 'problem' of Billy set the pattern we would follow throughout our marriage.

There were other signs during those first months we were together that our relationship was not what it should be. I see-sawed between wondering if I had done the right thing and trusting that, even if things weren't perfect, they would improve in time. Tony was neither a romantic man nor a very affectionate one, but I was young and so naive that the good times – and there were many of them – outweighed my doubts and uncertainty.

As we went into the new year, I felt settled. I had already mentally made a long-term commitment to Tony and set aside all thought of leaving him. When he bought a piece of land on which to build his dream house, I was pleased that he wanted to put down roots and excited by the prospect of working together on the house in which we would live.

But soon enough, I realised that Tony didn't see this as a joint project at all. He spent almost all his spare time in his study, drawing and redrawing plans for the house. He never sought my opinion and, when I offered it anyway, clearly didn't welcome my contribution. My uncle, a draughtsman, offered to draw up the blueprints, free of charge, but Tony didn't want his help. Night after night saw him hunched over his desk, measuring, drawing lines, erasing them in favour of another idea. Eventually I just left him to it, and my initial enthusiasm turned to acquiescence.

Perhaps I should have insisted that I wanted to be an equal partner in planning the house, but it was his money after all, so I came to accept the situation and busied myself with other things. Had I fought the small battles then, might we have avoided a bigger war later? I don't know, but the fact is, I allowed him to make decisions on my behalf, to cut me out – or perhaps I cut myself out. It took a terrible tragedy and months of counselling in later years for me to see what a fatal error we'd both made.

We moved into the house in October, when spring was at its loveliest. It was a beautiful and extremely comfortable home and I was content that we could start settling down, enjoy one another and our new surroundings. But my happiness would not last long.

In February 1987, Tony informed me that he had been transferred to Johannesburg. After just four months my comfortable life was turned upside down, and I faced a scary, unsettled future.

I tried to persuade Tony that we should stay in Durban. I tried hard, but it was useless. He had made up his mind to relocate without discussing his intentions with me, and it never once occurred to him to ask me how I felt about moving thousands of kilometres away. He automatically assumed that I'd go with him. We told my parents over lunch at my brother Nigel's house that we were going to Johannesburg. My father made the appropriate noises about his daughter leaving her home town and family to follow a man she wasn't married to, so we agreed that we would return to Durban a year later for a wedding on 27 February.

By April 1987, we were living in a cottage that Tony's company had rented for four months while we found our feet in Johannesburg. He soon settled into his job as financial director at Protea Surgical, a medical supply company, and I landed a job as a secretary at a company called Promix. I thoroughly enjoyed it, and our new life was both busy and happy. Tony was earning a decent salary, and weekends found us pottering around the garden together after plant-buying expeditions to one of the many nurseries. As dusk fell, I'd be watering the newly planted shrubs and seedlings and Tony would sit on the edge of the pool, his feet dangling in the

Tony

water, a well-deserved beer in hand. We fell into the habit of rewarding ourselves every Saturday night with two large, thick prime steaks that Tony would barbecue while I made salad and chips. We did this so many times that we finally got to the point where we decided we never wanted to see a steak again!

As promised, at the end of February 1988, we went back to Durban to get married, making the six-hour drive to my parents' home on a beautiful Friday morning. There was much excitement and I enjoyed all the attention, though I was a little nervous at the thought of the momentous event that would take place the next day. We went to bed early that night, in separate rooms, despite the fact that we had been living together for more than two years.

On Saturday morning, I awoke with joy in my heart. Ever since I was a little girl, I had dreamed of this day, and now it had arrived, and I could finally look forward to having children, building and nurturing a family. However small it was, my dream had come true, and I was happy.

Tony's parents had come from Zimbabwe, and his three sisters were also at the wedding – Jane from Australia, Penny and her husband Pip from England, Shelagh and her husband Chris from what was then called Bophuthatswana. My brothers Nigel and Bruce, with their respective partners, and friends and colleagues made up the rest of the hundred or so guests. The morning passed with a million things to do. Just after lunch I started dressing in the ivory-coloured dress that I'd had specially made. I wore flowers in my long, blonde hair, and Tony was in a dark-grey suit, bought at the last minute.

Driving to the church, I peered at the roadside pedestrians and wondered again if I was doing the right thing. I was happy to be getting married, but somewhere deep inside, still fearful of making another mistake. It was exactly four o'clock when I entered the Methodist Church in Durban's Musgrave Road. As I clutched my dad's arm and walked down the aisle, all my doubts disappeared. I saw Tony, smiling as he waited for me to take my place at his side, and was filled with happiness. My father kissed me and then, my hand safely clasped in Tony's, we faced the minister together.

We gazed into each other's eyes as we exchanged our vows. I followed the minister's words closely, and when I said 'I do' and 'till death us do part', I meant it from the bottom of my heart. Not even with hindsight would I believe anything except that the commitment Tony and I made that day truly was 'for better or for worse'. I was proud to become Tony's wife, and knowing that he loved me evoked a feeling of well-being, an enthusiasm for our future together, a sense that everything was possible.

We spent our wedding night at my parents' home. We had agreed that going to a hotel would be an unnecessary expense, and I would often tease him, in years to come, about spending his first night as a married man under his mother-in-law's roof. Early the next morning, we set off back to Johannesburg. We had both taken the Monday off and spent it with one of Tony's sisters, but on Tuesday morning it was back to work and business as usual.

We had decided to wait until we were more settled in our jobs before going on a honeymoon, but in the end we never did. Every so often we would promise one another that we would go 'next year', but then time would pass and other priorities would arise, so we just never got round to it. In later years, I became somewhat resentful that we had missed out on this component of the wedding ritual, but I lacked all power of persuasion where Tony was concerned, so throughout our marriage my role was to accept, to let it be.

Does that reflect on our inability to pay attention to small but important things? Were major decisions made without discussion between us? Should I have fought against exclusion and for the right to have my feelings and opinions taken into account? Sure – but at the time, I elected instead to avoid confrontation or be reduced to begging. Things are different now. I am far more aware of how important it is to sort out the small things, to assert my will and give voice to my wishes. I am independent in ways that I could never have been while married to Tony.

I understand that many people will influence and affect my life, but that I need to live by my own rules. Never again will I compromise my own needs. I will be flexible, certainly, but I will also do everything possible to avoid surrendering my comfort or desires in favour of anyone else's. This has been one of the hardest lessons I have learned, and it took a terrible, tragic loss to do so, but, in all conscience, it wasn't so much that Tony took my power and individuality from me as that I gave it up. It was my duty to look after myself and I don't think I did a good job of that at all. I believed that my first priority was to look after Tony. That thinking failed us both, but my sincere hope is that others might learn from my mistakes.

In deciding to have another child, I was bombarded with

the opinions, wishes and advice of many other people. I fully accept that there are sound reasons and a multitude of views that would influence others to choose a different route. I was told that it would be wrong, impractical, a bad idea, something I should reconsider at a later stage, even a sin. But in the end, I had to follow my own heart. It felt right for me to have another child, and to do so as soon as possible. I knew, above all, that getting pregnant was not a honeymoon I could put off year after year.

So, after much soul searching and discussion with those who love me, I made the decision to be a mom again, no matter what others said or felt. Many might have wanted different things for me. But the 'many' did not lose three children to a brutal death. Nor did the 'many' know the deep desire, the arms that ached to hold another child. Having a baby might well have been the wrong decision for 'many', but for me it was the right one, of that I am convinced.

What I was less sure of at the time was exactly how this would come about.

3

My children

TONY AND I HAD BEEN MARRIED FOR ABOUT A YEAR when we decided to start a family. It wasn't really a tough or complicated decision. We were married, thus children would follow, but that didn't mean having them was a casual decision. In fact, becoming a mother was everything to me, a role that consumed me and encompassed my every wish and all the meaning I ever found in life.

It was a time of great change in our country. Political parties were scrambling for position; there was social and economic upheaval; unrest was rampant and bombs were going off from time to time. The future was uncertain.

In 1989, Namibia, governed by South Africa for seven decades, began a one-year transition to democracy. Closer to home, teenage activist Stompie Seipei was abducted and later found murdered. PW Botha was ousted as leader of the ruling National Party and replaced by FW de Klerk, who wasted little time in opening the door to talks with the African National Congress that would see an end to apartheid and usher in majority rule. No one knew if the new political dispensation would bring peace and prosperity, or civil war and chaos, so there was an atmosphere of both fear and hope.

Tony and I had moved to Edenglen, east of Johannesburg. His sister Jane had recently had her first baby, and from time to time she and her husband would hint that it was time we followed suit, teasing us about when our first-born would arrive. One evening, as we sat on the patio having coffee, Tony suddenly said: 'So when are we going to start a family?' I replied that we were living in such uncertain and possibly dangerous times that I wasn't sure we should have children yet. In the days that followed, however, I realised that there never is a 'perfect' time to bring children into the world. Besides, I really, really wanted to be a mother, so Tony and I agreed that I would stop taking birth control pills.

I had been using oral contraception for so long that I thought it would take several months for my hormones to adjust and meanwhile the political scenario might become more positive. Did I have a surprise coming!

In April, I missed my period, craved popcorn and somehow knew that I was pregnant. When our doctor confirmed that I was expecting my first child, I was ecstatic. I was twenty-nine years old and felt on top of the world. Another of my dreams was coming true.

As soon as Tony arrived home I told him the news, and he was equally excited. We agreed that I would quit my full-time job in favour of temporary positions that would not only pay somewhat better, but would allow me greater flexibility of time. Coincidentally, my first assignment was with Acromed, a company that produced baby food! I worked three days a week and spent the rest of my time preparing for the baby or just contemplating the wonder of carrying a child. It was as if I was in another world. Life was beautiful and I never tired of talking about the baby, my pregnancy, what life would be like once our child was born. Everything else paled in comparison.

Tony was clearly thrilled at the prospect of becoming a father. Never one to share his thoughts and feelings, he seemed kinder during my pregnancy and treated me ever so gently. I knew he was as anxious for the baby to arrive as I was.

It was a relatively easy pregnancy. I had almost no nausea and was only uncomfortable towards the end. I continued working part time and ran the house as usual, shopping for groceries, taking care of Tony, buying all the things the baby would need. On a Thursday morning about a fortnight before my due date, I got up as usual and started getting ready to go to work. I had been going to antenatal classes regularly and Tony had also attended a few, but never having been pregnant before I didn't really know what to expect, so when I felt severe pains that morning, I decided to call the gynaecologist. The nursing sister at his rooms suggested that I come in for an examination.

It took him about a minute to confirm that I was in labour and immediately admit me to the Sandton Clinic, north of Johannesburg. I had read an article about a woman who became paralysed after having an epidural, so when a nurse asked if I wanted one, I said I would try to do without. I was so brave, and so naive!

The next contraction was altogether too painful for my liking, so I said I would like an epidural after all, please. Fine, said the nurse, the doctor would be there shortly to administer the drugs.

When a man came into the ward, introduced himself as 'mister' and said he was there to give me the epidural, I cringed and complained that I wanted a 'real' doctor to do it. To my embarrassment, he explained that he was indeed a doctor, and a professor to boot. Tony teased me afterwards about not having realised that some medical specialists in South Africa favoured the British form of address rather than 'doctor' once they reached a certain level of expertise, but all I knew at the time was that no one was going to do anything that might put my baby at risk.

The epidural worked for a while but, as my labour progressed, I wouldn't have minded another jab. Thankfully, it wasn't long before my beautiful, healthy son was born. It was 11 January 1990, and we decided to name him after his father and grandfather, though his first name was one that we both just liked. Kevin John Adlington was the most beautiful creature I had ever seen.

When they put that little boy in my arms, it felt as though my life had changed completely. Yesterday was gone and this was the start of a whole new era. Kevin had curly hair that was quite long and the face of an angel – don't all new babies? He was a skinny little thing, with a scrawny body and crinkled hands with the tiniest fingers and fingernails one could imagine. I was examining all the nooks and crannies of his perfect body when a nurse took him away to be bathed.

When he was brought back to me later, I was convinced that this was not the baby I had cradled in my arms before. His curly hair was gone! The nurses assured me that his curls had merely been flattened when they washed him, but I checked him out thoroughly nevertheless, determined to know everything about him that I could, so that no one would ever be able to fool me with a substitute! Years afterwards, when I needed that intimate knowledge of my son's beautiful body, I was in a coma and unable to point to all the amazing features that would help to identify him after he was murdered.

I wanted to go home the very next day. I couldn't wait to take care of Kevin myself. It was lovely to hold him in my arms, and I could hardly believe that I had carried him for nine months, or that he was mine. I was on top of the world.

Kevin was fair-skinned and had blue eyes, with a reddish tint to his hair. I thought he looked like me, but when I fed him for the first time, I noticed that he had a dimple on one cheek in almost the exact same spot as Tony. As he grew older, his eyes changed to hazel, but he kept his naturally curly hair. I loved combing and touching that hair.

My son was happy and contented. He loved sleeping, and sometimes I had to wipe his face gently with a wet cloth to wake him up and prod him to finish his bottle. For the first year of his life, all he did was sleep and eat. Often, he would fall asleep before I had even finished winding him, and from the age of twelve weeks he slept through the night.

Once a week we went to a clinic so that his weight and development could be monitored. When he was about four months old, I started him on solid food, all home-made. I remember that at first it was just pumpkin or squash with a little butter, and that I gradually added potato and other vegetables as he grew.

I had stopped working and it was lovely to be with Kevin all the time. I joined a gym, and every day I'd wrap my baby up in his pram and walk to my exercise session, parking the pram next to whatever apparatus I was using as I went through my hour-long routine. He was quite content to lie and watch me or take a nap. One morning, while doing step work, I noticed Kevin staring at me intently. He looked me straight in the eye and laughed out loud as I teased him, 'Yes, you little angel, this is what I have to do because of you!' Of course he hadn't understood a word of what I'd said, but the tone of my voice had obviously amused him. The image of that toothless grin is burned into my consciousness forever.

Tony loved Kevin. He was proud to be a father and especially happy that he had a son. The months after Kevin's arrival were some of the best and most intimate we ever had. It was during that time that I saw Tony at his gentlest and most tender. He was not emotionally demonstrative, but it was the closest he ever came to sharing his deepest feelings. When he came home in the evenings, he would greet Kevin before saying hello to me. He played with Kevin constantly, but drew the line at changing nappies or preparing baby food. Sometimes he would put Kevin in a baby seat on the carpet and lie in front of him, tickling the baby, talking to him and rocking the chair.

When Kevin was nine months old, Tony and I agreed that a second child would be great. We planned to have only two and wanted them close to one another in age. Within a month or two I was pregnant again, and, as with Kevin, I sailed through the experience, with no morning sickness, no problems and no cravings. Towards the end of the term my doctor told me I was having a girl. Though we didn't really have a preference, Tony and I were both thrilled that we would be blessed with a child of each gender. Our lives seemed as close to perfect as was possible.

My children

Katelyn was expected early in October 1991. However, when I saw my gynaecologist in the last week of August, he was concerned that she was in too much of a hurry to be born. He gave me pills that would stop or slow down the process if I went into labour early, as he wanted to give the baby at least one more week to develop before delivery.

A few nights later, we had supper and went to bed as usual. I had felt some discomfort and pain and, the doctor having assured me that they would not harm the baby, I took some of the pills as prescribed. After a while, I got up to go to the toilet, had a shower and made tea to pass the time until the pills went to work, but it wasn't long before I was doubled over on our bed in pain.

By 1 a.m. I knew it was time. 'Tony, I think we should get to the hospital immediately,' I said between contractions.

My neighbour Jenny had kindly offered to take care of Kevin while I was in the maternity ward, but things moved too swiftly that night to even think about waking her. As I reached the front door of our house, I went down on all fours in agony. I yelled at Tony to bring Kevin from his cot, his teddy bear and bottle. Tony was dutifully following my 'orders' and first had to get the baby seat from my car and put it in his. Even in the throes of labour, I would not allow Kevin – or our other children, later – to ride in the car unless they were strapped in. It felt as though everything was happening in slow motion, but after Tony had Kevin safely in the car seat, I tried to walk the few metres to the vehicle. I couldn't make it, and dropped down on all fours again. Tony jumped out of the car and came to help me to my feet and into the passenger seat.

We sped off and onto the N1 highway towards the Sandton Clinic, some twenty-five kilometres away. Tony put his foot down as I had never known him do before. I was moaning in pain, and as my water broke and I fought to breathe, I think he hit 180 km/h. Kevin was crying and I was trying to pacify him, saying, 'It's okay, boy, Mommy is okay.'

We screeched to a halt in front of the hospital and Tony jumped out. It was the wrong entrance! We sped off again, only to find that we were somehow in the wrong lane and separated from the entrance to the maternity section by a neatly manicured flower bed. Tony revved the engine and drove straight across the flower bed, gouging two deep tracks that must have infuriated a gardener the next day. He jumped out and ran into the hospital, calling for help. The nurses gave him a look that said: 'Stop panicking, calm down!'

He rushed back to the car and I told him to look after Kevin. I was between contractions, so I was able to get out of the car and walk into the hospital unaided. But as the next wave of pain hit me, I fell to the floor on my hands and knees again. Believe me, I wasn't trying to be dramatic – that really was the only position in which I felt some relief.

I felt an instinctive urge to place my hand inside my pants and hold on for dear life. I could feel my daughter's head, and screamed that the baby was coming. 'Where is the trolley?' a nurse yelled at Tony. 'I don't know, I don't work here!' he yelled back. The security guard manning the entrance made a beeline for the fresh air outside. I think the whole affair frightened him and he thought it best to play no part.

Someone found a gurney and helped me onto it. Tony had

put Kevin down and he was clinging to one of the legs as I was pushed towards the lift. What an Adlington circus!

The staff rushed me into the first available room and a midwife stripped off my unflattering tracksuit pants and T-shirt. She struggled with my takkies. I had tied double knots in the laces. 'How on earth did your wife get these tied like this?' she asked Tony. 'I don't know,' he answered. 'Cut them off!' I yelled. She did, and almost immediately, with Kevin playing on the floor and everyone else still frantic, Katelyn Ann Adlington was born.

The hospital had contacted Dr Peter Koll, the gynaecologist who had also delivered Kevin. His first question, when he arrived from an interrupted dinner party, was: 'Why is Mrs Adlington on a steel trolley?' Said one of the nurses: 'Doctor, with this little one there was no time, she was in a hurry to start her life!'

Dr Koll would later deliver Craig as well, but Katelyn pretty much did it all by herself. It was 29 August 1991, and for the rest of her life, my daughter would continue to hurry everyone along.

Kevin was fascinated by his sister, who looked exactly like him, but he was rather disappointed that she was so small. I suspect he had anticipated an instant playmate of his own size.

I really enjoyed Katelyn. With Kevin, I had almost wished the days away, impatient to track each stage of his early development. With Katelyn, I was more relaxed, knowing that she would do everything at exactly the time she was supposed to. Skinny like her brother, she was a tiny, dainty little girl. Her hair was dark at first but had turned blonde by the time she went to school, and she had a mop of it. When she was ten years old, this beautiful hair would be the only thing that allowed detectives to identify her charred and mutilated little body as that of my daughter.

Katelyn was still in nappies when we went to Zimbabwe on holiday to visit Tony's parents. For three days while we were there I was terribly nauseous and thought I was contracting flu. The symptoms cleared up, but once we were home again, my body started sending me signals that I recognised all too well. Dr Koll confirmed that I was pregnant again.

Deep in my heart, I was extremely pleased. Another child would be an unexpected gift, a final chance for me to see another little life develop. But I was worried about Tony's reaction to the news and about our financial situation. As I'd anticipated, he was less than overjoyed, and it took quite a while for him to accept that we were going to have a third child. He had quit his permanent job with Protea and was working freelance at the time, bringing home what I certainly felt was enough money to meet our needs.

But Tony was always driven and he had set himself the goal of becoming wealthy. He measured everything he did against that objective. Being financially successful was important to him, and though I did not particularly share his passion for making lots of money, I was happy enough for him to pursue his dream.

But I did feel that he was struggling to settle down. There were times when I genuinely forgot whom he was working for, but he always gave the impression that he was in control and doing what he wanted.

Our four-year-old marriage had found a comfortable rhythm, with me devoting most of my time to the children and Tony

My children

focusing on work, but things between us were both easy and pleasant. We were young, had two beautiful children and another on the way, and a long life ahead. In retrospect, I think Tony was really unhappy at the prospect of a third child, though – possibly even angry, and certainly worried about the financial aspect. But we never discussed his feelings, and I was so preoccupied with Kevin, Katelyn and my pregnancy that I didn't really take them into account. As with so much else, we simply failed to deal with our different views on a major issue.

Dr Koll was determined not to have a repeat of Katelyn's birth, so we agreed to induce labour at thirty-eight weeks. Unbeknown to me, Tony had contacted his father and had him explain all the emergency procedures he would need to follow in case the baby arrived unexpectedly and at home. Without saying a word to me, he had written everything down, just in case. But, at the appointed time, I was admitted to the Sandton Clinic again, a drip was set up and, within minutes, my water broke. As with Kevin, I initially declined an epidural, and by the time I changed my mind and asked for one, Dr Koll said it was too late, that the baby would be born before the effect kicked in. Instead, I was given painkillers that I had to inhale through my nose. With Tony beside me urging me to 'Breathe! Breathe!' I gulped down air on every one of his counts, until the doctor eventually told him to 'stop counting or your wife will pass out'.

Craig Anthony Adlington was the biggest of my three children, weighing in at 2.7 kilograms on 1 December 1992. He was a chubby little thing, which was lovely after the two skinny kids I'd had before, and was the spitting image of his father. It was impossible to tell them apart in baby photographs. I had secretly hoped for another boy, but I told no one and declined prenatal offers to learn my baby's gender, so our second son was a happy surprise.

Because the children were close to each other in age, it made sense for me to be a full-time mother rather than go back to work and pay someone else to look after them. I loved being with them. Every morning I would line up their bottles, twenty-one of them, and make them up for the day, trying to be as organised as possible. I enjoyed mealtimes the most. I would make them special treats and loved watching them eat. I also made all their clothes myself. We used to go for long walks and I would play with one while the others were sleeping. When Kevin was about three and a half, he started attending a playgroup three mornings a week. He loved it. I will always have etched in my mind an image of Kevin bringing me his little suitcase as soon as he was dressed. He couldn't understand that he only went to 'school' on certain days and he was so happy when he could.

During this time, I developed some wonderful friendships with other young mothers. I was closest to Karen Fouché, who lived nearby. We were about the same age, and she had blonde hair with blue eyes and a ready smile. She was funny and interesting and quite an extrovert. I loved her company and she became a really good friend.

We visited one another often and our families got on well together. That period of my life was just about as happy as anyone can expect when you are doing what you love best.

When Craig was seven months old, Tony came home with

My children

the news that he had been transferred to Cape Town. He was working for Galaxy Jewellers and had just returned from a business trip to Cape Town. Katelyn would soon turn two and enjoyed being part of a playgroup three times a week, while Kevin was thriving at his pre-school. I told Tony that I had strong reservations about disrupting their lives with a move, that I was settled and content with our lifestyle and our friends, but he had already made up his mind and refused to be swayed.

It seemed he had fallen in love with Cape Town on his trip and was sure that we would all enjoy living there. Besides, he argued, Galaxy's head office was in Cape Town and that was where he wanted to be.

In July 1993, the five of us boarded an aircraft to explore what would become our home and arrange accommodation. We found a house quite easily and returned to Johannesburg to pack up our lives. On a beautiful October morning, I watched the removal truck containing all our earthly possessions pull off and head for the Cape. Tony started our car and we drove out of our gates for the last time, followed the truck for a while, then overtook it and headed south.

I could never have predicted that Cape Town would become the city of my heart, the place where my children would go to school, where I would make lifelong friends – and where I would know my greatest trauma and sorrow. It also became the place I longed for when I was away, the symbol of my healing and, most importantly, where I would choose to live with my beautiful second daughter.

The decision to have another child was far more deliberate

and made with the benefit of much greater wisdom than had been the case with Kevin, Katelyn and Craig. As a married couple, Tony and I had had it easy, in a way. Everyone expected us to have children, we expected to start a family, and so it was. After Craig's birth I made peace with the fact that there would be no more babies. Having another child, without a husband, proved a completely different kettle of fish, especially since that choice came packaged with a huge number of obstacles. Previously, I would not have dreamed of becoming a single mother and dealing with all the issues to which the status exposes one. But I would never have guessed, either, that I would find myself facing enormous obstacles that would require all my strength to overcome.

As we sped towards Cape Town on that spring day in 1993, I stared out of the car window, filled with uncertainty about what the future held in store. A part of me was sad, but I was also excited at the prospect of new and unknown challenges.

Little did I know that I was heading for a place that would become home in the fullest sense of the word, only to lose everything that made it so, before slowly starting to carve out a meaningful life once again.

4
Hazel

THE ONE THING THAT MADE OUR MOVE TO CAPE Town easier was the fact that my friend Karen and her family had gone to live there a few months earlier. By the time we arrived, the Fouchés were well settled in the Mother City.

Our friendship resumed as if we had never been apart. We entertained our respective families and friends at each other's homes and our lives became closely intertwined. Karen and I shared our deepest feelings with one another. As my best friend and confidante, she knew my joys and fears and dreams, and I trusted her advice. I loved and deeply respected Karen, and the interaction between our families enriched our lives.

The children loved visiting the Fouchés, and Katelyn, in particular, adored Karen. Her sons, Matthew and Dane, were a little older than mine, but they all got along well. One Christmas, we all gathered at the Fouché holiday home on the Breede River. On a beautiful morning, we set off to cruise the picturesque river. Karen's husband Michael, Tony and all five delighted children were in a rubber duck – or dinghy – with Karen and me being towed behind in a large inflated inner tube.

Michael took off suddenly and quite fast. He turned around to look at us and saw Karen smiling, giving him the thumbs-up to go even faster, and me, next to her, petrified and frantically signalling a thumbs-down to go slower. The kids were shrieking with delight.

Another boat was approaching and, as it passed us, the wake washed over our tube, flipping Karen and me backwards into the water. I remember opening my eyes and seeing Karen's laughing face through the murky water. Her blonde hair floated around her head like an aura, her eyes were open and her mouth contorted with mirth. That happy image will never leave me.

My lungs were bursting and, as my head popped above the water's surface, I screamed with laughter. I saw my three children in the back of the boat, eyes wide, not sure whether they should be horrified or highly amused as they waited anxiously for a sign that everything was all right. As Karen bobbed up next to me, she yelled out loud and everyone relaxed and howled with amusement. We swam towards the dinghy, weak with laughter, and the children grabbed hold of our arms and legs to pull us aboard. What a happy day that was!

Karen and I saw each other regularly. We would shop for groceries together or take the children on outings. Often, we would meet for coffee and just chat – about our husbands and children, our hopes and dreams, our daily lives. We shared an interest in staying healthy and loved to pamper ourselves, and would see one another at the gym and the hairdressing salon. I had always been fussy about my hair, and I think it was through Karen that I discovered Shaun. Oh, if only we could understand the deep significance of a particular relationship when first meeting someone.

Shaun had his own hairdressing salon and personified every trite cliché about gay stylists. He was flamboyant, loud, strong, extroverted and a beautiful man, with long blond hair, a stunning smile and a fabulous body. People loved Shaun instantly. His personality was honest, whimsical and inviting. He played the stereotypical gay hairdresser as if the role had been written for him, but he had a deep sense of morality and caring for others that went way beyond a calling. He was sophisticated and warm and just when you thought you had him figured out, he would surprise you. He was also the best damn hairdresser on either side of Table Mountain!

Tony had settled into his job as financial manager with Galaxy and we had bought a lovely house in Long Street, Constantia. It was a comfortable home that will always hold happy memories for me. The kitchen was large and practical, and there were three bedrooms, as well as a loft room leading off the lounge. Craig slept there, with an intercom connected to the main bedroom. We converted the garages into a cottage that we eventually rented out.

There was a paved area outside the kitchen where Kevin and Katelyn could ride their bikes, and a good-sized pool where they spent their summer days. The front garden was quite pretty, and both Tony and I pottered about in it over weekends.

The children were developing distinct individual personalities. Kevin was quiet and confident, with a surprising sense of humour. Katelyn was a serious little girl, shy but kind and loving. Craig was pure sunshine. He loved everyone and everything.

As soon as we had established ourselves in the new house, the debate began about getting a dog. I wanted my children to grow up loving animals and knowing the friendship they can offer. Tony's family had always had miniature schnauzers, and he was keen on the breed. They are medium-sized dogs with short coats and above-average intelligence. Independent, boisterous and sometimes intolerant of other dogs, schnauzers make both excellent watchdogs and family pets. I had no particular preference for any breed; I just loved dogs.

While driving home one evening, I saw a litter of puppies

running alongside a busy street. I couldn't believe it, but they were schnauzers! As my car approached, they scuttled back to a gate and crept underneath to safety. The next day, they were on the pavement again. I got out of my car and rang the bell at the house from which they came. I told the housekeeper that the dogs were outside the property and could easily be run over. She fetched them, but twenty-four hours later they were back on the pavement.

This time, the mistress of the house answered the door. I explained my concern about the puppies and asked if she might want to sell one of them. She agreed, and I picked what I thought was the cutest of the litter. It was a seriously pedigreed little animal and I paid R600 for her, which was a bit steep, but I reckoned it was well worth it.

When I arrived home with the puppy, however, Tony gave her one look and said she had neither character nor personality. He wanted to see the rest of the litter. I was extremely hurt, but I took him back to the owner, where he exchanged the pup that I had selected for one of his own choice. I can't remember why, but he named her Hazel.

I liked her just as much as my original choice, but was bitterly upset that my gift had been rejected in favour of another. Tony's actions wounded me deeply. At that moment, he made me feel as if I could do nothing right. I showed some of my anger towards Tony and sulked for a while, even tried explaining my pain, but he simply shrugged it off. He did not tolerate lengthy emotional outbursts. In later years, this was one of the days that stood out in my memory as an example of our dishonesty in dealing with our emotions. Even in something as relatively minor as acquiring a puppy, Tony claimed it as his right to make decisions, while the feelings, opinions and ideas

Hazel

of others were of no concern. It was precisely this attitude that saw him decide when and how he would die and whom he would take with him, no matter the impact on anyone else.

For my part, I was simply incapable of making my feelings count. I had difficulty even getting Tony to hear me. I preferred to avoid conflict and, however much it hurt, I never put up much of a fight. I should have. Because we never faced these experiences honestly, we didn't grow from them. As was the pattern of our relationship, I soon buried my hurt and focused on the joy of having Hazel. The children loved her, I loved her, mother-in-law loved her, everyone did.

Hazel was a typical schnauzer. She was a stocky dog with a wiry black and silver coat, a characteristic droopy moustache and bushy beard. Her head was long, and she had distinctive eyebrows. Her dark, oval eyes seemed to hold a thousand stories and I adored her pointed ears.

Kevin and Katelyn loved teaching Hazel tricks and games. They would spend hours running after her, teasing her with a ball, shouting instructions, reprimanding her for not 'fetching', over and over again. Hazel took it all in her stride. She obeyed enough to keep the kids interested in the game but not quite enough to let them think the task had been successfully completed. She was a challenging pupil with boundless energy and was constantly with the children, in one of their beds or on the couch in the lounge. She was thoroughly spoiled, a full member of the family around whom our lives pretty much revolved. That never changed. We were besotted with her, and I loved her all the more for the way she taught my children to care.

They carried her around the house, washed and brushed her, stroked her and talked to her constantly, much as I had done with Billy, my cockatiel. Every morning before they left for school, Hazel got farewell hugs. Every afternoon when they came home, Hazel was at the gate, tail wagging, waiting to be picked up and petted.

She was very much a family pet, equally affectionate with all of us, which was one of the things that made her so special. A few years later, we bought Kevin his own dog, a Border collie that he named Jacky. He looked after her really well and became extremely attached to her, but unfortunately Tony became progressively more irritated by the damage Jacky caused to the garden. It seemed to me that he would often blame the dog for things she hadn't even done, and the situation became unbearable – a source of severe tension in our home. Tony shouted at Jacky whenever she was around, and before long she would run and hide as soon as she heard him arriving home. I tried as best I could to prevent the situation from becoming explosive, but I couldn't.

One day, Tony lost control and not only yelled at Jacky, but also aimed a kick in her direction. She ran for cover. He didn't injure her, but as I saw that beautiful animal slink away cowering, I knew that something had to be done. I was torn, because Kevin loved Jacky dearly, but I realised that Tony would never accept her. I talked to Kevin and explained that we would have to let Jacky go. I promised we would find her a good home, and we did. Afterwards, Kevin and I spoke about Jacky and the fact that we had been unable to keep her, but the matter was never again mentioned between Tony and me.

After a while we got another schnauzer, Henry. He became Hazel's best doggie friend and Kevin's special companion. Henry crept deep into my heart as well, but when it came to watching over the children, it was Hazel I relied on, more than any human being. When they went to the park a block from our house, I trusted Hazel to come running home if anything was wrong. On many an evening, I let them cycle in front of the house. As long as Hazel was with them, I felt at ease. I knew she would bark furiously if any stranger approached.

It is strange that such a small dog could give me such an enormous sense of security, but Hazel was synonymous with my children's safety. Sadly, on the morning that all three of them were bludgeoned and murdered, Tony had locked both Hazel and Henry up, leaving them to witness and sense the massacre, but unable to protect the children. The two friends were trapped in the family room. We were in the habit of leaving the glass sliding doors slightly open for the dogs to go in and out, but on the morning of the murders, the doors were firmly shut, trapping them inside. They must have sensed that something was terribly wrong, seen Tony carrying the children's limp bodies to the study, smelled the smoke and fire. The firemen found Hazel running berserk in that room, visibly and deeply traumatised. It took them ages to catch and remove the meekest, mildest fur ball on four legs.

Hazel and I had a special understanding when it came to the children. I expected her to always protect them from harm, and she rose proudly to the challenge. But when they needed her most, when they were in desperate and mortal danger, Tony deliberately shut her out, denied her the chance to save them. Ironically, in more ways than she could ever understand, the time would come when she would help and comfort me. In the end, I was the one that Hazel saved.

5

Decisions made, lessons learned

WITH ALL THREE CHILDREN AT SCHOOL, TONY AND I bought a coffee shop in Claremont in 1996. It had seating for about seventy people and a full-time staff of four, with two additional waitresses on Saturdays. In addition to serving beverages, cakes and burgers, we sold pottery, glassware and a small range of gifts.

The hours were long – from 8 a.m. to 5 p.m. on weekdays, until 1 p.m. on Saturdays – and in addition to running the shop, I had also turned the cottage on our property into a commercial enterprise. Our lives were busy and noisy and fast, like those of any dual-income couple with three children, but we had it all under control.

Katelyn went to Springfield Convent in Wynberg from the age of four until the end of Grade 5. I chose the school because it had a reputation for academic excellence. Established in 1871 as a parochial Catholic school, it welcomed pupils of all faiths. A high premium was placed on the teaching of truth and tolerance, and the sunny classrooms were set in wonderful gardens, with an extensive programme of outdoor activities on offer.

Katelyn was a lovely little girl who looked adorable in her light-blue dress with a white collar. School became her second home and she made many friends. It wasn't long before my Saturdays were spent ferrying her from one play date to another.

Katelyn was so happy at Springfield that I have already made plans to send my second daughter, Kylie-Ann, to the same school when she is old enough. It will be comforting to know that her little feet will follow in the steps of the older sister she never knew. Already I imagine her looking just as cute in her school uniform, hair neatly gathered in a ponytail, jumping and skipping along the corridors so familiar to Katelyn for six years.

Kevin started school at United Herzlia in Constantia. When we had relocated to Cape Town, a friend recommended the school, which was known for its emphasis on the holistic development of pupils. An added bonus was that the school was within walking distance of our house, so, although we were not Jewish, our little redheaded boy went there and fitted in beautifully. He liked it so much that, for a while, we observed the rituals of Shabbat on Friday evenings. Kevin looked forward all week to Friday, when not only was he given bread at school, but got to wear a little kippah, the round cloth cap worn by Jewish boys during prayers. I have tender memories of his red hair sticking out under his kippah.

From Grade 1 to the end of Grade 4, however, we moved Kevin to Diocesan College – or Bishops, as it is more generally known. The sprawling grounds at the foot of Table Mountain in the leafy suburb of Rondebosch and unique architectural style of the buildings make this one of South Africa's most attractive schools, but Kevin didn't do as well as we had hoped, and we decided to enrol him at Redham House from Grade 5. Craig joined him there after attending Jacob's Ladder pre-school in

Meadowridge and spending a year at Bishops. Both boys settled in well at Redham and enjoyed going to school.

Though separated by more than a thousand kilometres, I remained close to my parents. My mother stayed with us for a month or two after each of our children was born, and I tried to spend Christmas with them every year. They were fond and proud of their grandchildren, and we enjoyed spending time with my brothers and their families. The children loved the beach at Amanzimtoti and thrived on being spoiled by their grandparents. My parents respected my choices and our privacy and never interfered in our lives, but I confided in them a lot. When Tony and I were going through a difficult patch or struggling with a particular problem, I turned to them, as I had always done. At least once a week we spoke on the phone and I shared with them everything that was happening in our lives. I still do.

It was only in the agonising aftermath of the murders, when all of us were searching for answers, that my mom and dad told me they had often wondered whether Tony and I should not perhaps have separated. My mother confessed that, at times, she had sensed that he was unsettled. She had also noticed that he was quite domineering and that I had fallen into a pattern of mostly doing as he wanted without question, so as to avoid his anger or outbursts of frustration.

My parents also realised that there was something unauthentic about Tony, and had difficulty pinpointing exactly who and what he really was. It seemed they never felt entirely comfortable in his presence, and this feeling grew stronger over the years as they witnessed him overreacting to minor incidents.

Once, when we were visiting them on holiday, Tony bought a newspaper and a magazine. While he sat at the table browsing through the newspaper, my father picked up the magazine and started paging through it. Tony became extremely agitated and rushed into the bathroom, where I was having a relaxing soak. We still had more than a week of our holiday to go, so I couldn't believe my ears when he said, 'Come, pack our things, I have to get home.'

My parents remained calm and quiet as we packed, said our goodbyes and left. Tony made no attempt to explain or apologise, but somehow we all knew that he'd cut short our visit for no other reason than that my dad had looked at the magazine before he had. After that, no one ever touched any reading matter that Tony bought, whether he was at home or not.

We celebrated the dawn of 1996 at a party with friends. Neither Tony nor I ever drank much, so the few glasses of wine we had that night went straight to our heads. It was a fun-filled evening and, when we arrived home, we laughed our way to bed and made love. A few weeks later, I woke up one morning with the overwhelming certainty that I was pregnant. I grabbed a calendar and worked out when I'd last had a period. We had made love at the most crucial time of my cycle. My mind was in turmoil. Instinctively, I was overjoyed at the likelihood of another baby, but I had a nagging anxiety about what Tony would make of the situation. I decided to say nothing and wait another two weeks. When my period didn't arrive, I told Tony that I was almost certainly pregnant. He looked at me and said firmly: 'No, you are not.'

I kept at it. 'Tony, I've missed my period, we made love at the most critical time, I'm convinced that I'm pregnant.'

He would have none of it, as if saying that it wasn't so, made it so. 'No, you're not. Stop saying that.'

I made an appointment for a pregnancy test. Tony would cover for me at the coffee shop for an hour or two, but he kept saying I was foolish to take the test, that the pregnancy was all in my mind. Around 5 p.m., as I was closing the shop for the day, my doctor rang and confirmed that I was, indeed, carrying a baby.

I didn't know what to feel as I drove home. By the time I walked into the house, I was weeping uncontrollably. I put my keys down and looked at Tony. He looked back at me and, without either of us saying a word, he understood immediately that we were expecting a fourth child. When he spoke, it felt as if my world was collapsing around me. 'You have to have an abortion.'

'Tony, I can't!'

He was insistent. 'You have to. You cannot have another child. We cannot have another child. I don't want another child. We are not having this child.'

With a single word, my husband had shattered me. Abortion? I had never considered one, even for a second. 'I can't do it,' I said again.

But Tony was adamant. He had spoken his mind and, as far as he was concerned, the deed was as good as done. Not another word was said. There was no discussion of my feelings about the pregnancy or an abortion, or how we would deal with one. The only thing I was sure of at that moment was that Tony would not change his mind. He had been reluctant enough to accept my unplanned third pregnancy and had no interest in another child. Even after Craig was born, it took a while for Tony to accept him. Thankfully, my sunshine child had worked his magic and his father did come around in time, but there was no chance of that happening again.

I called my parents. I cried. I kept asking myself, 'What do I do? What do I do?' I went to my doctor's rooms every evening for a fortnight in search of answers. I would close the coffee shop and just arrive at the surgery. My doctor saw me every time, listened to me sobbing and making the same argument over and over, and never charged me a cent, bless him.

Inevitably, the doctor's advice was that Tony and I needed to talk about the situation, but Tony would not discuss it again. As far as he was concerned, abortion was the only solution and that was the end of it.

When I turned to my mother for guidance, she reminded me of a friend who had fallen pregnant before she was married and had an abortion. For years, for decades, this woman mourned that child. My mother not only knew me well, but also agreed with me that while everyone should have the right to choose, I would find it all but impossible to live with a decision to abort.

'Whatever you do, don't do this,' she advised. 'Do not go through with it. You will have to live with that decision forever. Whether or not Tony wants another child, you have to think of yourself and figure out what *you* want and can cope with. Whatever happens, we will support you fully.'

I felt trapped. I knew how fortunate I was to have three beautiful children already, but I also knew that there were many women who would give anything to have a baby, and I felt sad and resentful that I had a husband who expected me to put an end to a life that had just begun. The unspoken pressure from Tony was enormous. I knew instinctively that if I refused to terminate the pregnancy, my marriage would be over. That thought frightened me terribly. I loved Tony and our children adored him. The consequences of refusing to have an abortion would be devastating, but I didn't have it in me to agree.

Eventually, my doctor referred me to a colleague at the Kingsbury Hospital in Claremont. I went to see him and explained my horrible dilemma. I wanted to know how much time I still had to make a final decision, hoping that even another week or two would help me find the courage and clarity to make the best choice. After questioning me closely, he said: 'Look, please stop crying. Let's do a scan and see how far along you are before we talk about the various options.'

The scan over, he came and sat beside me and took my hand in his. 'Mrs Adlington, you may be spared the decision. This foetus is about to abort at any time.'

It was as if the whole of Table Mountain lifted off my shoulders! I wouldn't have to make the decision after all. Yes, I would lose the baby, but not through any conscious act on my part. Nature, or the severe stress I had been under, had freed me of that burden, and while I still thank God that the decision was taken out of my hands, my relief at the time was mingled with feelings of great sadness and resentment towards Tony.

I was admitted to hospital almost immediately for a D&C (dilation and curettage). During the procedure, under general anaesthetic, my womb would be scraped, thus automatically ending my pregnancy. It was a fairly routine procedure and I would be able to go home six hours afterwards.

Tony went with me. While I filled in the various hospital forms, he sat in a chair near the reception desk. I gradually became aware that he was tapping one foot impatiently. On and on ... tap, tap, tap! He became even more irritated when the clerk turned away from us to answer a ringing phone, tapping that foot and looking at his watch. 'I have a lawyer's appointment. I can't be late,' he said.

It was just too much. 'Tony, please – just take your briefcase and go. I'll fill in the forms and take myself off to wherever I need to be. Please, just go.'

He stood up, took his briefcase and left. I followed a porter to my room in tears. I honestly couldn't believe that he had walked away and left me there alone. It was the poor doctor who had to calm me down. He probably thought I was being overemotional, and maybe I was, but I felt abandoned and overwhelmed by both sadness and anger. Another woman who had just lost a baby was surrounded by her family. She was crying, her husband was crying, their parents were crying and I was crying inconsolably. If I had been there for a voluntary abortion, I knew that at that moment I would have got up out of the bed and walked out. I could never have gone through with it.

When they came to take me to the operating theatre, I was still sobbing. Not only was I deeply disturbed about the loss of a life that had started forming in my body, I was also terribly hurt by Tony's departure and wracked with guilt that the tension between us might have triggered the miscarriage. I couldn't help but think that it was my fault the foetus was not viable.

When Tony fetched me from the hospital later, we barely spoke. He took me home, then went to buy takeaway food for supper. I went to bed early. Hazel crept onto the bed and came to lie with me. Her small, warm body brought me comfort and she stared at me for a long while, her gentle eyes telling me that she felt my sadness.

Tony and I never spoke about the baby we lost. There was simply no reference to the experience, ever, but our relationship was never quite the same again. We went through some truly awful patches, then things would improve somewhat, only to hit a bad phase again. I was silently resentful, to a degree that

I'd never been before, and Tony sensed it. He retaliated by becoming increasingly abusive, both verbally and emotionally.

After the murders, one of the newspapers described Tony as a Jekyll and Hyde personality, but the truth is, until that last morning, he never hurt me physically. He did develop a habit of walking past me and lifting his hand as if he was going to slap me, but he tried to pass this off as 'a joke'. The first few times it happened, I got quite a fright. Later, I pretended that it didn't bother me, hoping that if I ignored the gesture, he would stop, but he just kept on doing it, apparently enjoying my reaction, whether it was fear, anger, irritation or silence.

Non-physical abuse had become part of my life long before the miscarriage. It happened sporadically and almost always coincided with particularly tense periods, such as when Tony changed jobs, was having difficulties at work or was frustrated that things weren't going his way. He always had to feel in control – of situations, people, even the most trivial aspects of daily life. The smallest thing could send him into a verbal rage, directed at me. What I hated most was that he would yell and shout at me in front of the children, and his anger made them both scared and submissive. I didn't want my boys to grow up thinking this was how to treat a woman, or Katelyn thinking that she had to accept that kind of abuse from any man, but I felt powerless to do anything about the situation.

Karen was the one person with whom I shared my misery. Thank God for a friend like her! I remember calling her one day and saying, 'I feel like climbing into my car and driving off the cliff at the top of Chapman's Peak.' She listened to all my problems with sympathy, but her advice was always the same: 'Don't say that. Things will come right. Give it some more time.'

In partnership with his mother, Vicky, Shaun had opened a

gorgeous salon, Moments in Time, in Claremont. I remember being shocked by the image that stared back at me from a mirror on a visit soon after the miscarriage. My face was drawn, my eyes dull and lifeless. Shaun saw it too, and asked in his gentle, caring way: 'Now what's wrong? Where has the pretty gone?'

'I am so tired,' I answered, but it was all I could do to stop myself from bursting into tears. The thing was, despite Karen's reassurances, matters were not getting better at home. If anything, Tony's angry outbursts were becoming more frequent and my unhappiness was mounting. I became especially concerned that he seemed to be more involved in Kevin's life than in Katelyn's or Craig's, yet could be utterly cold and unfeeling at times. He had always refused to take part in any school activities, but now he started promising Kevin that he would. On one occasion there was a braai at Kevin's school for the pupils, who could each take along one parent. Tony insisted that he would go, and for days before he built up Kevin's expectations with endless references to the fun they were going to have together.

On the day of the function, however, Tony came home from work and, without offering any explanation, announced that he was not going. 'But you promised, Dad!' Kevin cried. It made no difference. Despite our eldest son's tears, his father simply refused to keep his word. It fell to me to take his place alongside an extremely upset and bewildered boy that evening.

Tony's lies and broken promises continued to the very end. More times than I can remember, the children would become aware that some or other international pop star was coming to Cape Town, and Tony would say: 'We're going to the concert. I am definitely getting tickets, don't worry.' He never did. The shows would come and go, leaving three greatly disappointed children with some lame excuse about why he had not kept his word.

Where Tony caused harm by refusing to acknowledge, let alone discuss, problems, I was guilty of sacrificing my needs and wants to his will, even when this was to my detriment. I did that when I lost Billy, when I allowed him to shut me out of planning our house in Durban, when he took back the puppy I had chosen, when he cut short our family holiday, when I unexpectedly fell pregnant, and so many other times. In the worst and final instance, I was totally excluded from his decision to take my children from me.

I make my own decisions now, however hard that is. Never again will I fall into the trap of letting other people's views and desires shape my life. My enforced independence came at too high a price to be surrendered, and another marriage or the influence of any man in my daughter's life is not something I am ready to deal with. Maybe I never will be again.

Having another child was undoubtedly one of the most important decisions I have ever had to make. I was a single woman over the age of forty, and it was never in my nature to have sex with a stranger, or even someone I knew, for the sole purpose of falling pregnant. Besides, one of the consequences of what I had been through was that I was in no way ready or able to form a new relationship, however good it might be.

But I did want to be a mother again, more than anything – not to replace the children I had lost, since nothing could ever do that, but to lavish on another child, a different child in a new life, all the love I have to give. Once I made that decision, there was no stopping me. Scared or not, I needed to find a doctor who would perform artificial insemination. That was my solution, and I made the first available appointment.

6

Life changes

WHEN TONY KILLED HIMSELF AND OUR CHILDREN, it was generally thought – even by the police – that he was facing huge financial problems. Since he never discussed money with me and actually refused to do so, I had no way of knowing whether or not this was true. However, I was aware that his assorted business ventures had run into trouble at various times, because when things weren't going according to his plan, he made our lives hell.

Always restless, he explored many different ways of earning a living, some more successful than others. He didn't want to work in the corporate world, yet was unable to deal with the erratic income and demands of entrepreneurship. Even when he had three lighting shops and was bringing home a substantial amount of money each month, he wasn't satisfied and sold them to start something else.

Tony always seemed to be looking for a bigger and more lucrative source of income. Each time his search failed, he became more abusive, lashing out at me in anger and alternating between indifference and playful generosity towards the children. He would creep into their rooms on his hands and knees just as they were dropping off to sleep and scare them silly. The kids loved it and would scream and laugh with joy, but I found Tony's game far less amusing. It always took a while for the children to settle down afterwards, and in the morning it was left to me to deal with fractious youngsters suffering from lack of sleep.

At times, Tony could also be malicious and downright dishonest. Once, when we were in a shop to buy a portable radio, he took a pack of batteries off the shelf, tore it open and put the batteries into the radio to test it. No one else saw him do this, and when he went to pay for the radio, he said nothing about the batteries. I walked out of the shop in dismay and we had a terrible argument in the car. Tony treated his theft of the batteries as a joke and could not grasp that I saw nothing funny about his behaviour.

Another time, while we were still living in Johannesburg, we were waiting our turn in a butchery while a woman was buying meat. While the customer placed her parcels in a shopping bag and wasn't looking, the butcher put her change – several cash notes – on the counter. The next thing, the woman asked where her change was. The butcher insisted he had put it on the counter, where Tony was standing, and even asked my husband if he had not picked it up by mistake. Tony denied any knowledge of the money.

I walked out of the store in silence that time, too, and we had a raging row. Tony continued to deny that he had pocketed the money, but I was certain he was lying. I said he'd done a cruel thing, because the woman had had a child with her and that might have been the only money she had to buy food. He didn't care and found it hilarious that I thought he was a thief.

I never told anyone about the incident. I would have been

Life changes

too ashamed to show my husband for the selfish, uncaring person I came to realise he could sometimes be.

Apart from his final act of self-serving brutality, perhaps the most devastating thing that Tony ever did was sell our beautiful home in Constantia without a word to me. We had lived there for six years, and the children and I had woven our lives around friends, schools, activities and neighbours in the area. One evening, I came home to Tony's blunt announcement that the house had been sold, the deal signed and sealed.

I was absolutely heartbroken. Not a word or suggestion had passed between us to indicate that he was even thinking about such a drastic move, and he offered no explanation after it was done. I suppose he acted out of financial desperation, but I was shocked, frustrated and deeply wounded that I knew nothing until it was too late. Confronted with an irreversible situation, I had no option but to move, though I never forgave him for what he did.

To make matters worse, he left it to me to explain this upheaval to the children. It proved impossible for me to hide my feelings from them, but my tears served only to anger Tony, who launched a series of deliberate actions that would hurt me even more.

On one of our last Sundays in Constantia, I spent the entire morning preparing a roast for lunch. I went to a lot of trouble, hoping that a family meal would ease some of the tension and lift hearts that were heavy with the sadness of leaving our home. About half an hour before the food was ready, I saw Tony driving towards the gate with all three children in the car. I ran outside and told them that lunch was almost ready. He said he'd be back in a few minutes after fetching something he needed from the shop.

When they returned, the children all had cold drinks and had gorged themselves on sweets and crisps. None of them felt like eating. I couldn't believe what Tony had done, but when I looked at him, I could see the spite and satisfaction in his eyes.

This was one of far too many times in my marriage when I felt angry, helpless and beaten. Whenever it happened, I would withdraw into myself and find a quiet spot where I could lick my wounds and try to understand what was happening, why we were so unhappy. Then a new day would roll around, the normal rhythm of our lives would resume and on we'd go, until the next time.

Early in 2000, we moved to a rented house in Marina da Gama, an attractive development bordering Muizenberg on the False Bay side of Cape Town. The marina curls around the eastern shore of Zandvlei lake, with many of the houses having water frontage. Surrounded by mountains and abundant with bird life, the area offers tranquil living, and many of the residents have small boats that allow them to explore the waterways so distinctive of the suburb.

My life had been turned upside down, but the house was comfortable and I did everything possible to turn it into our new home. But I remained angry and frustrated, and needed something more. We had sold the coffee shop after two years, as the hours were long and I wanted to spend part of my day at home with my children. So, when Kevin came home one afternoon with the news that his school was looking for someone to run the tuck shop, I jumped at the chance. My experience at

Life changes

the coffee shop obviously counted in my favour, and after a few meetings at the school, I was handed the keys to the Redham House tuck shop.

We opened for business five days later. Open from 7.30 a.m. to 4.45 p.m. on weekdays, our busiest times were the two half-hour breaks, when hundreds of pupils lined up to buy beverages, toasted sandwiches, cake, sweets and snacks. There was also a steady stream of customers in the afternoons, when the pupils played sport.

Kevin was at the age where he mostly pretended not to know me. He loved the bacon and egg sandwich we made, however, and I would give him a subtle wink as I passed one to him.

Craig had no such inhibitions. He loved the cheese sandwich and would just march into the tuck-shop kitchen to get one, until I started giving him money and made him stand in line like the rest of the kids. From his place in the queue he would shout, 'Mommy! Mommy!' to get my attention, and as I passed him a sandwich, he would say, 'Love you, Mommy,' then go off happily to eat and play. Some days things were really hectic, and I wouldn't even register that I was serving Craig until I heard the familiar, 'Love you, Mommy.' If necessary, he'd repeat it, but he never left until I had responded, 'Love you, Craigie.' Naturally, some of the boys turned this into a joke, and as soon as Craig said 'love you', a choir of voices would reply, 'Love you, Craigie.' It didn't bother him at all. He was at that wonderful age when his mom was the centre of his universe, and no amount of teasing was going to change that.

I loved the tuck shop, which not only kept me busy while I

was still adapting to a new home and environment, but also let me 'mother' dozens of children. I introduced smoothies for the girls and weaned a number of the older boys off stodgy meat pies by offering them a healthy breakfast instead. I created a huge amount of extra work for myself and ended up exhausted at the end of each day, but it was worth it.

Little did I know that I was on the brink of a crisis that would knock my feet out from under me.

Soon after our weekend at the Breede River with Karen's family, she developed a throat irritation. Initially treated for tuberculosis, the problem persisted, and she sought a second opinion. That didn't help either, and finally she was referred to an oncologist. One Thursday morning I dropped in to see how she was doing and heard her telling someone on the phone that she wanted her test results. When she hung up, Karen was in tears. The person she had spoken to had refused to tell her anything, insisting that she should see the doctor the next day and that someone should go with her.

Karen knew immediately that something was seriously wrong. She asked me to phone Michael and tell him to organise his schedule so that he could accompany her to the doctor's rooms at 10 a.m. the next day. All Michael said before he slammed the phone down was: 'Oh my God.'

Karen had lung cancer, and the doctor told her she had only months to live. Michael went to pieces, but Karen was strangely calm at first. Throughout that day, I wanted desperately to call her and find out what the doctor had said, but I couldn't find the courage to dial her number. When I got home there was a message to call her, and I did.

Life changes

'Are you sitting down?' she asked. 'You won't believe what I have to tell you. I have only a few more months to live.'

The next day, Tony and I left the children with friends and drove to the Fouché house. Michael and Karen both came out to greet us, but when she and I went into the house, he stayed in the garden with Tony and broke down, sobbing. It was absolutely awful. After a while, the two men came inside and sat down at the dining-room table, saying little. Karen and I sat in the kitchen. Over and over, she repeated that all she was asking for was ten more years, so that she could see her two boys through school. After a while, as though she was trying to strike a bargain with an unseen force, she said nine years would be enough … then it went down to eight and seven and six. I had never felt so desperately sorry for anyone.

It was, I think, during that sad conversation that I truly realised how precious life is, that it is a gift to be cherished, but one that can be lost in the blink of an eye. Many, many months later, the whisper of a newborn baby's breath on my cheek would remind me of that realisation, and I would give thanks anew for the enormous privilege of being alive and healthy and able to share my world with friends and family.

Karen was thirty-seven. Her sons were twelve and nine. In the nine months that followed the devastating diagnosis, she was constantly on my mind, and I spent every possible moment with her. The cancer was unforgiving and her condition deteriorated rapidly. Before long, she was on high doses of morphine to ease the pain, but even with the drugs, she often woke up screaming and moaning in agony. When it came time for her to be admitted to a hospice in Kenilworth, she was as frail as someone three times her age, her body wasted to skin and bone. Another friend and I took turns going to the hospice to feed her, but she hardly ate anything any more. Towards the end, I spent almost entire weekends at her bedside. She would beg me not to leave her and I would stay as long as I possibly could.

On one of the rare occasions that she went home for a while, I knelt down in front of her to put her slippers on while Michael went to bring the car around. She was sitting on the edge of her bed, thin as a rake, her legs dangling motionless. Suddenly, she put her arms around me and clung to me with what little strength she had left, sobbing pitifully.

'Debbie, I can't believe how quickly I've become so weak. I just cannot believe it,' she cried.

More than anything, it was the thought of leaving her children that upset her. 'I can't believe this has happened to me. I just cannot believe that I am going – that I am leaving my boys behind. That I'm leaving Michael behind.'

Oh God, it was horrible to see someone suffer like that. I could not come to terms with the fact that my dearest friend was going through so much physical and emotional pain.

Karen died on 9 June 2000. Another friend phoned to tell me and to say I needn't go to the hospice that day as planned. I went all the same. This was the first time someone so close to me had died and I needed to see for myself that Karen was really gone.

Her passing filled me with a deep sadness. I missed her constantly, and for some time afterwards I would reach for the phone to call her and tell her something. Then I'd remember that I'd never again hear her say, 'Debs, it's me. How are you? Do you guys want to come over?'

Life changes

I didn't know it then, but it must have been around this time that Tony's problems started mounting. Even if I had not been mourning Karen's loss, he wouldn't have shared his concerns with me, and I had no inkling that he was on a slippery slope. Of course, I knew that our marriage was nowhere near perfect, but evidently he was also facing financial pressure and had made some really bad decisions. I will never know if he was worried about the future and how to provide for three children, whether he was overcome by a black depression that affected his judgement and perspective, whether he considered leaving me but was unable to do so, or feared that I might leave him. We never once discussed divorce, but some years earlier, during one of our many altercations, I had said that I sometimes felt like leaving him. Tony replied: 'Don't think that you can take the children,' but that was the closest we ever came to any talk of splitting up. Needless to say, had I known then how our marriage would end, I would have paid far more attention to the implications of his warning.

As it was, whatever he was feeling in the second half of 2001, he elected not to share his anxiety with me or any of his friends, retreating instead to what must have been a desolate and tormented mental house of horror. Once or twice during that period, I woke up during the night to find Tony standing at the foot of our bed, staring at me. When I asked what was wrong, he turned away in silence or answered, 'Nothing, go back to sleep.' For all I know, he was imagining what it would be like to carry out the diabolical plan that I believe he was already forming in his mind.

When the schools closed for the summer holidays in

December, I'd been running the tuck shop at Redham House for two years. It had been decided that one of the teachers would take over the shop in the new year, and although I knew I'd miss it, there was nothing I could do. I sold the equipment and appliances that I had installed and decided to wait until January before embarking on anything new. The children and I were leaving for a holiday with my parents two days after Christmas and there would be time enough when we returned to find something that would keep me busy.

As had happened occasionally before, Tony was going to stay at home on account of his workload at the real estate franchise he had bought. The previous December, the children and I had flown to Durban and he had joined us later, travelling by bus. The children had been so excited when he told them about his trip that they insisted our next journey should be by road.

While at Amanzimtoti, I told my parents that I wasn't really happy, that Tony and I had constant disagreements and had grown apart in many ways. They suggested that if I was so unhappy, perhaps I should consider a divorce, but I knew even then that I'd never do it. Whether this was because I couldn't or wouldn't accept that my second marriage had failed, like the first, or whether I was simply too scared to go it alone with three children, I can't be sure, but no matter how bad things became, I would not have left Tony.

Karen's death had taught me to accept what one cannot change and reminded me that there are many forms of suffering. In some ways, her loss prepared me for what was yet to come. Her greatest concern had been for the welfare of her sons when

Life changes

they lost their mother. I understood her pain in this regard completely, and appreciated the time I had with my children all the more. I had always been openly affectionate with them, but when I held them now, I felt a definite connection and was flooded with love and gratitude that three such wonderful little beings were in my life. I will be eternally indebted to Karen for helping me to realise anew, and just in time, how very precious Kevin, Katelyn and Craig were.

During the months I spent in hospital recovering from my physical injuries and emotional trauma, Karen was always on my mind and became a huge inspiration. Ghastly as they were, my physical wounds were nowhere near as excruciating as what she'd had to endure, and I always had the prospect of recovery, while she'd had none.

I often called on her to help me. In the chaos of my thoughts and feelings after the murders, the only sliver of comfort I found was knowing, believing with all my heart, that my children were with Karen. I remain convinced that she watches over them just as surely as I keep an eye on Dane and Matthew, who have grown into wonderful boys of whom she would be immensely proud.

When sadness colours my day, as still happens quite often, I find consolation in the certain knowledge that Karen, Kevin, Katelyn and Craig are together. My beloved children are with my best friend, and that means they are safe, and deeply loved.

7

The last twenty-four hours

OUR BEDROOM WAS FLOODED WITH SUNLIGHT WHEN I awoke on the morning of 15 January 2002. I opened my eyes and rested them on the curtains blowing gently in the breeze, touching the bed. Tony was already up and had opened the window. I could hear the familiar sounds of our house. The kids were chatting, one calling out to Hazel.

I let my mind wander to the lovely holiday the children and I had spent with my parents. We had been in Amanzimtoti for about two weeks and had arrived home only a few days before. Tony had telephoned and spoken to the children every night while we were away. They talked about the bus trip and what they had done during the day, but his conversations with the boys dealt mainly with the quad bikes he had promised them for Christmas. One of those calls had produced the only jarring note of our holiday.

The subject of quad bikes had come up some weeks before Christmas. Tony kept talking about them, bringing home pamphlets, driving past showrooms where they were on display until Kevin and Craig were quite beside themselves with excitement. I warned Tony not to raise their hopes, but he was adamant that he was going to get them each a bike.

There were no quad bikes under the Christmas tree or in our garage by 27 December, when the children and I left for Durban. Tony told the boys that they were on order, so naturally, whenever they spoke to him from my parents' house, they were anxious to know if the bikes had arrived. As had happened so many times, he had one excuse after the other, and one night I realised that Kevin had seen through the charade. When he put the phone down after speaking to his father, he told me he knew that Tony was not going to keep his word and that he didn't believe there would be any quad bikes.

When Tony fetched us from the bus station on 10 January, the boys asked again about the bikes. Tony said something vague about the wrong models having been delivered or the paintwork having been damaged. Kevin didn't mention quad bikes again, his silence bearing testimony to the fact that he knew he could not trust or believe his own father. It saddened me immensely that this had happened.

The children still had a few days of leisure, but soon we'd have to start getting ready to go back to school. Kevin and Craig would need new uniforms, since we had decided to take them out of Redham House and enrol them at Wynberg Boys' Junior, which had a name for discipline and academic excellence. I had no idea that Tony apparently didn't have the money to kit the boys out or pay their school fees, let alone that the cheques he'd written to pay the fees for the last term of 2001 had bounced.

Lying in bed that morning, I replayed in my mind recent conversations with my parents about the state of my marriage. I had told them I was confused and unhappy, but still believed I had made a commitment for life. More than anything, my

The last twenty-four hours

concern was how the children would be affected if we were to divorce. I wouldn't even know how to start talking to Tony about a separation, so I just had to trust that we would get through the latest bad patch.

I supposed that we would have to talk about moving, probably soon. Tony had told me before Christmas that he had a house in Kenilworth on his books that we might be able to live in, rent free. While I was in Amanzimtoti, he told me one night that he'd had a fight with the agent for our house at Marina da Gama, but had not gone into detail. As with the school fees, it would be several weeks before I knew that he had defaulted on our rent.

It didn't take the children long to realise I was awake. Katelyn jumped onto the bed and asked if she could spend the day with her best friend, Jessica. She loved sleeping over at Jessica's house and often went to church with the family on Sunday mornings. She'd come home bubbling about how much she had enjoyed the service and the rituals. In due course, I would find peace in knowing that the memorial service for my children was held in the very church Katelyn had liked so much.

Hazel jumped up on the bed as well, pushing her nose against my arm to signal that she wanted her head stroked. I turned her on her side and then on her back and shook her gently, tickling her tummy while her feet playfully careered up and down in the air in a million tiny steps.

After coffee and a shower, I drove Katelyn to Jessica's house in Constantia. We arranged to talk on the phone later to decide if Katelyn would spend the night. Craig and I went grocery shopping and got home around mid-morning. While

I washed the breakfast dishes and tidied the house, Tony and Kevin went off in the car. To my astonishment, they came back with a music centre for Kevin. I asked Tony how much it had cost, and he said R1 600. When we were alone, I told Tony it was madness to spend so much on a gift, but he just shrugged and said Kevin had wanted it. Later that afternoon, Kevin told me the truth. The music centre had actually cost R2 500.

A few days after the murders, my parents had a call from Hi-Fi Corporation. Tony's cheque had bounced. My father packed the music centre in its box and took it back to the store. When he explained what had happened, the manager refused to take the goods back and wrote off the debt.

Kevin spent the rest of that Tuesday afternoon in his room with a friend, Robert, playing CDs on his shiny new music centre. As usual, Craig and Hazel were happy just to be near me while I read for a while. Tony had gone out again after lunch, saying he had some work to do at the office. Around 6 p.m. I was surprised to see him pull into the driveway with Katelyn in the car. Without a word to anyone, he had gone to fetch her at Jessica's house, despite the fact that she had decided to sleep over after all. He'd told Jessica's mother that she needed to go home and tidy her room. Katelyn was quite upset, but it seemed best to calm her down and not make an issue of Tony's actions.

Looking back, I wondered if Jessica could have been my daughter's salvation. If Katelyn had stayed the night as planned, if the girls had not been home when Tony arrived, if Jessica's mother had phoned me to confirm the arrangements before Katelyn got into the car, would my daughter still be alive?

The last twenty-four hours

Rational thought says not, that her father would probably just have waited another day … or two, or three, but this remains one of the many questions that won't ever be answered.

While I made chicken, potatoes, vegetables and a creamy mushroom sauce for supper, I could see Katelyn and Tony playing a board game she had been given for Christmas. He seemed completely relaxed. There was nothing, not a single sign, that less than twelve hours later, my husband and all three of my children would be dead. I still find it unspeakably abhorrent that he sat there laughing with his daughter when he must already have made up his mind to kill her before the night was out. No matter how long I live, I will never comprehend the grotesque normality of those final hours.

It must have been around 7.30 p.m. when we sat down at the five green place mats on the dining table for what proved to be our family's last supper. Conversation flowed easily as we ate: Tony asked the children how they had spent the day, Kevin spoke about his time with Robert, Craig said he'd gone 'hopping' with me. He couldn't say 'shopping' when he was little and his baby word had become part of the family vocabulary. The children helped me clear the table and do the dishes and then asked if they could ride their bikes outside for a while.

Tony went to the study and I finished cleaning up the kitchen. I decided to let one pot soak overnight, filled it with water and placed it in the cupboard below the sink. Weeks later, my mother teased me about that pot, saying: 'Thank you very much indeed for leaving me the dirty pot to wash.' All I could say was: 'Well, I had to give you something to do, didn't I?'

From time to time, a yell or a laugh drifted into the living room from outside. I wasn't at all concerned about the children. The weather had been wonderful all day and the lingering dusk had not yet turned to dark. Besides, Hazel would bark if anyone came near them.

At nine o'clock, with their holiday bedtime approaching, I called them in. They parked their bicycles in the garage, showered, put on their pyjamas and came to say goodnight to Tony and me. I kissed each of them and gave them permission to read for a while, promising that I would come and tuck them in and turn out the lights. Kevin and Katelyn loved reading, while Craig paged through his picture books with gusto.

Kevin's bedroom was on the opposite side of the house from ours. The walls were a sunny yellow, the curtains and duvet cover a cheerful green and white check. He was still awake, lying on a red sheet, his matching pillow tucked under his head, when I went to settle him for the night. His favourite CD by the Backstreet Boys was playing on his new music centre. I switched it off, he turned onto his side and I tucked the duvet in behind his back and kissed him on the cheek. As I left, he was pulling his beloved bear – simply known as 'Kevin's Bear' – under his chin.

In Katelyn's room next door, I knelt down to kiss her. We had thrown out her bed, as it was falling apart, and had not yet found a replacement that we liked. Meanwhile, she was quite happy on a mattress on the floor. Her book, *Dream Pony*, had fallen onto her chest and her pink teddy was cuddled in one arm. I bent over to kiss her and she whispered sleepily, 'Good night, Mommy.'

The last twenty-four hours

Craig's room was next to the study and closest to the main bedroom. He was already fast asleep, lying on his tummy in the middle of the bed. He was still so small, had such a lovely, chubby body. Tomorrow, he'd have to do some more 'hopping' on those little legs, I thought. I moved him so that his head was resting on the pillow, stroked his hair, kissed him and drew the covers up over his shoulders. Hazel was sleeping at the foot of his bed. I picked her up and carried her to the kitchen, whispering to her and playing with her ears. Tony was still in the study. I put my head around the door, told him the kids were all asleep and that I was going to bed. The last word I heard my husband say rolled off his lips easily, quietly: 'Okay.'

After a long, relaxing shower, I opened the bathroom window as usual to prevent damp permeating the walls. Several weeks earlier, I'd had varicose veins surgically removed from one of my legs and it still hurt from time to time. That night it was especially painful, so, as I'd done a few times before, I pulled a camping mattress out of the cupboard where it was stored and rolled it out on the floor next to our double bed. By stacking pillows at one end, I could keep my leg elevated, without disturbing Tony.

I lay down on the makeshift bed, my head and shoulders propped against the wall, and flipped through a magazine until I felt my eyelids growing heavy. I fell into a deep sleep and don't know if Tony came to bed at all. My mother later said it looked as if the bed had been slept in, but Tony would have closed the bathroom window and the detectives found it open, so I doubt he went to bed that night.

Around 5 a.m., I awoke and went to the toilet. The house

was quiet and I wondered idly why Tony was already up. I had to be up by seven to open the door for our domestic worker, Maria Charles, so I propped myself up against the pillows and lay back on my mattress, watching the early light creep across the sky.

I don't know if I dozed off again or whether I was in that semi-conscious state between sleep and awakening when Tony came into the bedroom with the axe in his hand. I would have flashbacks of a silhouetted figure moving towards me, his arms raised above his head, holding something that aroused in me a sense of extreme danger, but the picture was never clear. I was told that when I was in hospital, the monitors went haywire every time a male nurse with cropped hair, tinted glasses and a build like Tony's came near me. My reaction to his presence was evidently so severe that he was told not to attend to me. I was also told that soon after regaining consciousness, I drew a picture of a man holding an axe above his head, but I never saw the sketch and have no recollection of being frightened of the nurse.

For a long time, I blamed myself for not trying to fight my attacker off or defend my children, but even if I had been wide awake, I don't think there was anything I could have done. If I'd realised what was about to happen, shock and fear would almost certainly have paralysed me. If I had tried to get away, Tony would have been between me and the only exit, and he was much stronger than me. If I had screamed or tried to run, it is entirely possible that I would not have survived the attack at all.

Tony hit me three times on the right side of my head with the edge of the axe. I don't remember feeling any pain, so the first blow must have rendered me unconscious. I do remember hearing several loud bangs at some point and being overcome by the realisation that something terrible was happening. I had a distinct sense of doom and an urgent need to make sure the children were all right, but I was unable to move.

I was found lying on my back against the pillows, blood streaming from my shattered head into the bedding and mattress. I don't know if Tony came back into the room or why he left me there and closed the door, thus preventing the smoke from the study from reaching me. I believe he left me for dead, but I won't ever know if he deliberately excluded me from the funeral pyre he set, ran out of time, didn't move me because I was too heavy to carry, or simply didn't care.

As far as the forensic experts could tell, he went to Kevin's room next, delivering several blows with the axe to our sleeping son's head. The red pillowcase turned dark as blood seeped into the fabric, flowed over the wooden bed frame and dripped onto the carpet below. The blows were so intense that the walls and the cupboard on which Kevin's brand new music centre stood were spattered with blood.

Katelyn loved sleeping on her tummy and she must have slipped off her pillows during the night. Tony hit her three times with the axe, shattering her little skull and defiling her bedclothes with blood and brain matter. Craig must have been lying on his left side, facing his father as he brought the axe blade down on his head once … twice … three times. It has remained my fervent prayer that my youngest son was dreaming of something gentle and beautiful and that he lost consciousness with the very first blow.

With me and all three children incapacitated, Tony had the time he needed to complete his monstrous plan. One by one, he wrapped a sheet or duvet around the children's mortally wounded bodies and carried them to the study. Their blood marked his path along the grey-tiled passage to where he stacked them one on top of the other, with Kevin on the floor and Katelyn sandwiched between her brothers.

Then Tony poured petrol over the children and on a pile of our most important documents and family photo albums, which he must have moved to the study some time during the night. For some inexplicable reason, he took the empty white plastic container back to the garage, where police later found it, complete with a bloody palm print.

It was impossible for investigators to reconstruct all of Tony's actions, or the sequence of events in those early morning hours. What was clear, however, is that somewhere between 6.30 and 7 a.m., he entered the study for the last time. Facing his three children, Tony Adlington, aged forty-nine, picked up his cigarette lighter and thumbed the tiny, corrugated silver wheel to release a small orange flame. He brought his hand down to allow the fire to lick a splash of petrol, and must have seen the flame thirstily consuming the stream of inflammable liquid he had poured.

At that moment, my husband made the final decision of his life. He lifted his hand to his forehead and placed the cold muzzle of his 9-mm Star semi-automatic pistol against his flesh. With flames leaping around his feet, he squeezed the trigger and catapulted a bullet into his head. An autopsy would show that it shattered part of his frontal lobe, midbrain and left cerebellum before exiting through his neck, and that death was instantaneous. The absence of any soot or smoke in his lungs confirmed that Tony was dead before he fell to the floor and landed on his stomach just centimetres away from and at right angles to his children.

For the rest of my life, I have to live with the knowledge that my children were not yet dead when they were carried into that study. Soot and smoke were found in all their airways, which meant they had continued to breathe for some time after the fire started. When I learned this, I could only beg God not to have let even one of them regain consciousness and see, hear or comprehend what was happening.

As he fell, the firearm spilled from Tony's grip and ended up under his legs. As the flames consumed the study, the last four bullets in the magazine exploded, loud bangs cleaving the early morning air in a neighbourhood just beginning to stir. Somehow, those four macabre salutes to the dead penetrated my consciousness. I heard them then and I still hear them today, distinct and clarion sounds of mortal danger.

One of our neighbours heard the shots as well, and looked out of a window to see smoke and flames billowing from the roof over the study. Another neighbour later told my parents, the police and the media that she had been disturbed by the sound of a child calling out before she became aware that our house was on fire. It terrifies me to think that Kevin's cries for help, which had echoed in my mind in hospital, might have been real after all.

Based on the autopsy reports, I can't believe that any of the children could have regained consciousness, even momentarily, after the horrific head injuries they had suffered, but, again, I will never know for sure. I have prayed incessantly that they knew nothing of the smoke and fire that engulfed them, that their last living memory was of being kissed goodnight and tucked in by the mother who adored them, and that they knew nothing else until they saw Karen's familiar smile, her arms outstretched to enfold them with love and safety.

    I take comfort from a vision of my best friend gently cupping the faces of my beloved children in her hands, softly crooning words of reassurance to soothe their sadness and confusion at knowing that the father they loved had taken them from the mother who would gladly have given her own life in order to save and protect them from harm.

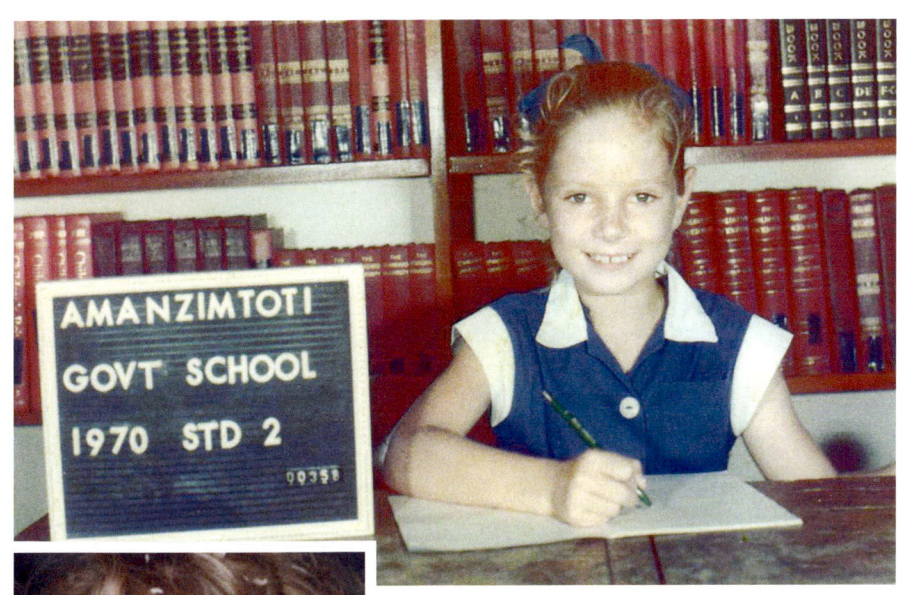

I was a happy little girl at primary school in Amanzimtoti, KwaZulu-Natal

Radiantly happy on my wedding day on 27 February 1988 in Durban

During a special christening we had arranged for our children at our home in Johannesburg. Tony holds Kevin, and Katelyn is in my arms

A lunch with friends. My best friend, Karen Fouché, is on the right of the picture, and Glynis Fish in the centre. Karen had already been diagnosed with cancer

Tony, Kevin, me and Katelyn in my parents-in-law's garden in Harare, Zimbabwe, during a family visit

Katelyn was furious with me for dragging her into a photographer's studio in Johannesburg, but Kevin took it all in his stride

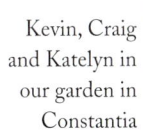

Kevin, Craig and Katelyn in our garden in Constantia

Kevin and Craig at home in Marina da Gama. This picture was taken a few months before their deaths

The house in Marina da Gama

Tony

The morning after: people were sent in to rescue what remained of our belongings. The number 19 is forever engraved on my mind

Fire damage at the house

My younger brother, Bruce MacInnes, in the burned-out study in which my children and husband had died

Friends helped my parents and brothers to move our belongings from the house in Marina da Gama into storage. I would not open the boxes for another eighteen months

At a memorial service for the children. From left: my older brother, Nigel MacInnes, Dad, Aunty Phyllis, my friend Isobel's mother, Mom, and Delecia and Keith Merrington, family friends who were incredibly supportive in the weeks that followed the murders

School friends of Kevin's and their mothers console each other at the memorial service. I was still in a coma in hospital

A bunch of flowers bears silent testimony to the tragedy at our house

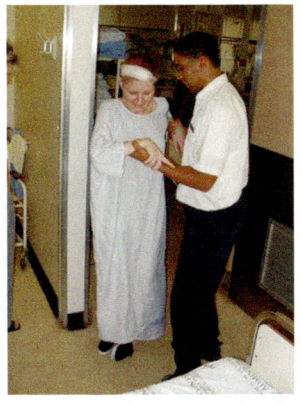

My first steps, with the support of my 'torturer', Frankie. It may have been only a small step, but it was a giant leap for me

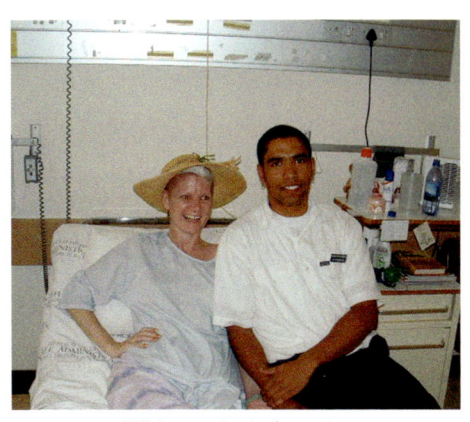

With my physiotherapist, Frankie, in Groote Schuur Hospital

With my parents, David and Margaret MacInnes, shortly before I left the hospital room that had become my 'home'. I would recognise those curtains anywhere – I stared holes into them

The opportunity to meet and thank the emergency crew, fire fighters and air rescue services occurred at a specially arranged gathering shortly before I left Cape Town for Amanzimtoti. Here I am talking to rescue team members Michael Smith (left) and Gustav Arndt

Looking forward to
the birth of my daughter

My new business at the
Blue Route Mall in Tokai

With Kylie-Ann,
December 2005

The angel in my life:
Kylie-Ann

8

Code Red

THE CALL FOR HELP WAS ROUTED TO THE OTTERY Fire Station at 7.04 a.m. When our neighbours saw smoke and flames escaping from the roof of our house, one of them dialled 10111, the emergency number. They acted fast and set in motion a chain of events that probably saved my life.

The fire station was a few kilometres from Marina da Gama. Three crews of fire fighters, in two fire engines and a rescue vehicle, were despatched to our house. The first fire truck arrived within seven minutes of the call being logged.

One of the first five firemen under command of a station officer to reach the house was Craig Crown. The tall, well-built leading fire fighter, with his shaven head and friendly smile, must have struck a professional picture as he climbed out of the rescue vehicle responding to a 'house on fire' call. Craig had answered hundreds of such calls in his fourteen years as a fire fighter. His days were spent in service of others. He was accustomed to dealing with serious trauma in motor vehicle accidents, burn victims, cats stuck in trees and raging factory blazes. After so many years on the job, a kind of 'routine' urgency had set in, and he knew exactly what to do.

His vehicle carried emergency rescue equipment, the Jaws of Life and special fire extinguishers. Craig's first task was to scan the scene and determine what had to be dealt with. He rushed to the gate, his eyes already taking in every detail of his surroundings.

Craig noticed the neighbours tirelessly spraying water from a garden hosepipe into the study of our house. He was conscious of the ever-present danger whenever there is fire – the fact that people might be trapped inside the building.

The ceiling and roof of the study had burned away. Large orange flames were leaping skywards above the walls. Flames had already started spreading to the adjoining structure. The fire was moving fast.

The fire fighters leapt over the padlocked gate, only to find the front door and security gate firmly locked as well. Their trained eyes spotted a small window and they kicked it in, aiming their hoses through the opening in the direction of the flames and turning on the taps. A white stream of water forced its way through the black pipes into open space and met the orange flames in mid-air.

As the rest of the crew fought the fire, Craig made his way to the front of the house, searching for another way in. He knew that there could be people sleeping inside, perhaps overcome by the smoke. Time was of the essence, and he moved with controlled urgency. His hand touched the sliding door to the patio and, applying pressure, it opened. He ran inside and unlocked the front door.

The fire fighters rushed into our home. Black smoke had started filling every room and there was little visibility. Their aim was to get as close to the core of the fire as possible. They set up the hoses again, spewing clouds of foam into the flames, attacking the fire with force in the hope of bringing it under control as swiftly as they could. The reality was that the blaze was raging fiercely and there was a very real danger that the entire house could be razed.

Protocol demanded that Craig search the premises. He found all the interleading doors closed and opened them cautiously as he made his way deeper into the building. The first bedroom he entered was my son Craig's. Fire fighter Craig immediately recognised it as a crime scene. The bed was empty and the duvet missing, but the bloodstained pillow and sheet told a disturbing tale.

Similar scenes greeted him in two more bedrooms. He knew that something terrible had happened and immediately radioed his suspicions to the station commander. What concerned him most was that these were obviously children's rooms.

As he entered the main bedroom, he saw me lying on the floor. He later explained that, at first glance, it seemed to him that the top of my skull was simply gone. Brain matter was clearly visible and blood had caked my hair to form bizarre red strands. His trained eyes saw no sign of life. There was no noticeable breathing, moaning or small movements as can usually be discerned in even critically injured people, and the wall behind me was spattered with blood. Craig had no doubt that I was dead, and felt certain that there had to be more people in the house. Where were those who had been hurt in the other bedrooms? He checked the cupboards, knowing that scared children often hide in them when at risk. Finding nothing, he stepped into the adjoining bathroom.

He noticed the open window, but found nothing more.

As he turned to leave the room and continue his search, something caught his eye. He looked around and his heart started racing. Was it real? Instinctively, unbelievingly, he blinked his eyes. He followed the movement of my bloody hand with a combination of horror and surprise.

The five fingers were spread slightly apart and the hand passed through the air, slowly waving in front of my face, palm outwards, as if to fend off some invisible enemy.

Craig dropped to his knees beside me. A section of my skull had split open, as if a small bomb had exploded within. He could not believe that I was alive, but, jolted into action, he called for assistance on his radio. Grabbing the bag containing basic life-support equipment, he reached for the bandages, drips, oxygen mask and cylinder. He wondered whether the 'golden hour' – the first crucial sixty minutes after someone suffers severe trauma, when the chances of saving a life are most favourable – had already passed.

Fire fighter Wayne Brink joined him. An oxygen mask was quickly connected to the cylinder and placed over my nose and mouth. Pure oxygen was forced into my lungs – vital assistance in any emergency, and especially where there are head injuries. The body in trauma claims all oxygen to keep the vital organs alive and a diminished supply to the brain can result in serious, often permanent, damage.

Meanwhile, the firemen had brought the blaze under control and confronted the devastating scene in the study. The message they relayed to the fire station was grave: 'We have one male adult, two male children, one female child, all deceased. We request police assistance.'

They also sent a Code Red message about a female adult. This meant that the injured patient was in a critical state and required immediate and advanced medical assistance, including evacuation by helicopter.

Craig started an intravenous drip to replace the fluid I had already lost and checked my vital signs. My breathing was shallow, my pulse indiscernible and my blood pressure had dropped to a point where death was almost inevitable. As the fluid from the drip seeped into my veins, my blood pressure began to stabilise. I was moaning and trying to speak, but the fire fighters couldn't understand what I was trying to communicate. Craig asked me my name and I became agitated. He said afterwards that it seemed I wanted them to leave me alone. He held my hand and spoke gently to me. 'It's all right, we are here to help you. You're safe, don't worry.'

While waiting for the helicopter and paramedics to arrive, Craig did what he could to stabilise me for transport to Groote Schuur Hospital's emergency room. He opened a multi-trauma dressing the size of a towel and laid it next to me. This he sprinkled with sterilised water to moisten and prevent it from sticking to the exposed brain matter. It was vital to stop contamination of the wound and any further blood loss.

Craig then slipped his gloved hands behind my neck and lifted my head slightly, slid the dressing under my head and drew the two sides over my face to enclose my entire head. Blood immediately began seeping through the plastic lining, and he had to apply a second, then a third dressing.

The paramedics arrived and took over at this point, mercifully injecting me with a strong analgesic that knocked me out before they intubated me. Craig rhythmically squeezed the airbag to help me breathe, while his colleagues placed a collar around my neck to protect my spine in case it had been injured.

The medivac helicopter had landed in a cul-de-sac at the end of our street, and as soon as the paramedics judged my condition stable enough for transportation, I was lifted onto a steel stretcher and wheeled towards the waiting chopper. The medical personnel who had treated me doubted that I would survive the ten-minute flight, and sometimes, in the worst and darkest moments, I have thought that it might have been better if I had died, given the horrific truth that I would learn a few weeks later. But I didn't, and on the good days I am grateful for that.

Inspector Willie Reyneveld from the detective unit at Muizenberg Police Station was in a meeting when he took a call from the Ottery Fire Station, requesting a detective at the scene of a house fire that involved fatalities. It took him twenty minutes to get to the address, and the first thing he did on arriving at 8.30 a.m. was to ask the most senior officer present for a report. The emergency personnel had found a family photograph in the living room and assumed that it was of the dead and injured.

Reyneveld walked from room to room, taking in the gruesome scenes in the children's bedrooms and following the bloody trail to the study. As he passed the main bedroom, Reyneveld saw the paramedics working frantically to stabilise me, and he told me later that he was convinced I was close to death. My pupils were fixed, my eyes wide open and staring upwards.

He also told me that he would never forget his first sight of the study. Most of the desk had been destroyed by the fire; the safe and filing cabinet were barely recognisable. The computer and all the books and files on the desk were badly burned or utterly destroyed. The floor was a mess of charred documents and photo albums mixed with water from the fire hoses. The record of my family's life – ultrasound scans of the children in my womb, class pictures, snapshots of celebrations and holidays, school reports, financial documents, birthday cards and crayoned drawings, all gone, obliterated as if none of it had ever happened. Then Reyneveld saw the bodies.

Tony had fallen behind the desk chair. Only the burned and matted tangle of Katelyn's remaining hair identified her as a little girl. The boys were lying next to her. The terrible head wounds were clearly visible, big, awful slashes where the axe wielded by their father had fallen.

It would be up to Reyneveld to piece together what had happened. He hoped that I would survive and be able to shed some light on this gruesome tableau, but he didn't really believe that I was going to live.

The police took photographs and videos of everything, inside the house and outside, while they waited for ballistic and forensic experts to arrive. Every detail was important. Because it is impossible to know at the initial stage of an investigation what might turn out to be crucial evidence, the detectives simply consider everything significant, and meticulously measure, gather, seal and mark every object at a crime scene.

It was patently obvious to the experienced inspector that he was, indeed, dealing with a crime, but of what nature? Had this family been attacked by intruders? One of the neighbours told Reyneveld that he had heard several distinct gunshots, and initially it was thought that all five of us had, in fact, been shot. But by whom? The police combed the garden, looking for marks against the walls where someone might have jumped over, broken branches or suspicious footprints, cigarette butts, drops of blood, anything that would indicate the presence of someone other than family members.

But the only signs of forced entry were those left by the firemen. The open window in my bathroom was not large enough for anyone to climb through, and the front gate had been secured with a heavy chain and padlock. The first neighbours on the scene had jumped over the wall to turn their hoses on the fire and the firemen had had to cut the padlock with bolt cutters when they arrived.

The police had no way of knowing at that point that we never locked the gate. It didn't even have a lock, but evidently Tony's planning had included the purchase of both a lock and a chain, which he must have used to secure the gate some time during the night.

The investigation team bagged and recorded everything – blood samples and spatters on the walls, ash particles, stray hairs, fingerprints, the empty petrol can, anything that would add a fragment to the macabre jigsaw puzzle they would have to assemble. They went through drawers and cupboards in search of clues about the identity of the victims, took statements from the neighbours and a deeply distressed Maria Charles, our domestic worker who had arrived around 8 a.m. to find the property swarming with police and emergency personnel.

In the midst of his investigation, Reyneveld heard our phone ring and answered the call. It was a friend of mine, hysterical after hearing a radio news report about the bodies of a man and three children being found in a house in Cannon Island Way at Marina da Gama.

It was after 5 p.m. when Reyneveld and his team left the house, still baffled by what they had found. The next morning, Reyneveld's first port of call was the mortuary at Salt River, where a pathologist took him by surprise, but also offered the first breakthrough in the investigation by telling him that only Tony had been shot. The children's injuries were not consistent with gunshot wounds, she said, but appeared to have been caused by a sharp, heavy object.

Nothing fitting that description had been found the day before, so Reyneveld and his team went back to the house to search anew. The study was still under water, turned murky by the ash and charred remains of the fire. After searching the rest of the house in vain for the murder weapon, the policemen donned gumboots and prepared to focus their efforts on the study. Just then, Reyneveld got a call from the forensic unit. The blood spatter in the bedrooms did not appear to be the result of gunshots, he was told. They should look for something sharp and heavy.

The inspector telephoned Maria. She was at home and still in shock, but she had worked for us for more than three years and was extremely fond of the children. Reyneveld suspected that she would do anything she could to help solve the dreadful mystery of what had happened to the family.

He asked if she knew of any object in the house, perhaps an ornament, that was sharp and heavy and could be used to kill someone. She said she had noticed, some weeks earlier, that Tony had bought an axe and placed it near the barbecue outside. Later, Maria saw that he had moved the axe into the study, but she never touched it and Tony never said anything about it.

I hadn't seen or known anything about the axe, and it was chilling for me to learn from the police that Tony had bought it on 2 December – the day after Craig's ninth birthday, when we had all gone to the Spur steakhouse in Tokai for a family celebration. They also established that he had bought the container of petrol on 4 December, which meant that he had decided to wipe out his family at least three weeks before we boarded a bus to go and visit my parents. All through the festive season, during all the telephone calls to the children at Amanzimtoti, whenever he spoke to the boys about quad bikes, for at least six weeks, my husband was planning and preparing to commit the most heinous acts imaginable, and I had had no idea.

Once the police knew what they were looking for, they pumped the water out of the study and found what remained of the axe. The wooden handle had burned away, but the solid iron blade was intact. Laboratory tests showed that it was smeared with blood, brains, and hair and bone fragments from the children and from me. Twelve times Tony had raised that axe above his head and brought it down with all his strength to shatter the heads and lives of the people he loved most.

Once the study was drained, the police also found the gun he had used to shoot himself.

By that point, Reyneveld was almost certain that he was

dealing not with a vicious attack by unidentified outsiders, but with a particularly gruesome family murder. DNA tests confirmed the identities of the four bodies found in the study and that the children and I had been bludgeoned with the axe.

The only question that remained, as far as the police were concerned, was why? An extensive probe of our financial situation turned up no evidence of fraud or other criminal activity, but it did become clear that Tony had fallen deeply into debt. The 'fight' with the Marina da Gama agent that he'd mentioned to me turned out to have been because he had defaulted on our rent and had, in fact, been served with an eviction notice. The only reason we were still in that house was because, while I was away, he had sold a lounge suite and used the money to secure four more weeks of occupancy. I had not even noticed that the furniture was gone, as it was in an extension of the house that we almost never used and which I had not been into since arriving home.

Tony had also sold one of our cars, an elderly Mercedes that I usually drove. I'd found that out when he fetched us after our holiday in the BMW that we had bought from Karen's husband, Michael, after she died. Tony never told me why he'd sold the car, just said he'd 'make a plan' to get another vehicle by the time the children went back to school. Over the next few months, other debts came to light as well, but I still have difficulty accepting that Tony thought the situation so dire that his only way out was the one he took. I can only think that he believed he had painted himself into a corner from which there was no other escape but death, but not even that explains why he killed the children.

Though my parents had raised the question of divorce during our holiday, I had said nothing of this to Tony, so he couldn't have thought he was about to lose the children or me. Although he never shared his fears and feelings with me, I cannot understand how he committed to a plan of murder and suicide as a 'solution'. For him to have made such a drastic, final and gruesome decision, he must have been in an unbearable, torturous and inescapable psychological state.

What I have never understood is how Tony was able to function so normally while his 'solution' took shape, especially during the six days after the children and I had come home from Amanzimtoti. The only problem I was aware of – and that had been in November, before we'd gone on holiday – was that he had been listed at a credit bureau for non-payment of R2 206 to Autopage. Subsequently, I also learned about the school fees that were in arrears, the rent row and that he had skipped payments on the BMW for three months. That came as something of a shock, as he had told me when we bought the car that he had paid Michael the full amount in cash. It transpired that WesBank had actually financed the deal and, when Tony defaulted, they threatened to repossess the car. My father paid the outstanding balance, thus allowing me to keep it. I was deeply grateful for his help, as not only had this been Karen's car, but it was also the last vehicle I rode in with my children.

While in no way trying to downplay the seriousness of the debt trap Tony was in, I can't help thinking there must have been some other way that we could have dealt with it, if only he had taken me into his confidence. But that, perhaps above all, was the fundamental problem throughout our relationship:

he never had. Even when his father died in 1995, he couldn't share his feelings with me, though the only time I ever saw him cry was immediately after his mother had telephoned to tell him the sad news. After that, however, he just clammed up and never spoke about his father again.

If he knew, during our last weekend together as a family, that he was going to carry out his plan on the morning of Wednesday 16 January, he gave no sign of it. Kevin had turned twelve the day after we got back from Amanzimtoti and, as with Craig's birthday, we went to the Spur in Tokai for supper. Tony gave every impression of being a happy dad when the waiters brought Kevin's cake, adorned with sparklers, and sang 'Happy Birthday' as cheerfully as the rest of us.

On Sunday 13 January, Tony woke up in a splendid mood and asked: 'So what should we do today?' By mid-morning, we were on our way to Hout Bay, where we spent several hours at the World of Birds. The children loved the monkeys, and after lunch we took them to the curio shop, where Kevin and Craig chose key rings for their promised quad bikes.

How we moved from such relatively mundane family outings to the carnage that abruptly halted life as I knew it, I won't ever comprehend. The mental image of Tony cradling each of our severely injured children in his arms as he carried them to the study will haunt me forever. The thought of my babies lying one on top of the other, inhaling the smoke as the intense heat of the flames licked at their perfect little bodies, is more painful than I can bear. I will always wonder if Kevin really did cry out for me, or whether I'd heard him do so only in my mind. I am tortured by the fear that one of them had been conscious, however briefly; that Katelyn, always a light sleeper, saw her father coming at her with an axe; that they felt the pain as their father delivered those vicious blows.

When those thoughts come, unbidden, to my mind, I have to force myself to remember that my children are now where they can never come to harm again; that any horror they might have known that morning was but a moment in their short yet happy lives.

Mercifully, as I was wheeled from the helipad to the trauma unit at Groote Schuur Hospital, I was oblivious to the fact that the bodies of my husband of fourteen years and my three beloved children were being moved from our house to a waiting police van. Nor did I know that our home was filled with strangers prying into every intimate detail of our lives in search of answers. Many of those involved in my rescue and the investigation sought counselling afterwards. They said the brutality of the attacks was among the worst they had ever encountered in their careers.

As I was rolled into the trauma unit I had no idea, either, that Hazel was howling incessantly, running from one side of the family room to the other, utterly terrified and traumatised. By the time the firemen managed to catch and calm her, the remains of the four people who had pretty much been the sum total of my reason for living were being placed on icy slabs at the Salt River mortuary. I thank God that I never had to see them there.

9

Survival

THE TRAUMA UNIT STAFF CHECKED MY VITAL SIGNS and applied a fresh dressing to my wounds, both to contain the bleeding and to prevent infection. A few floors up, neurosurgeon Dr David Le Feuvre's team was already preparing to receive me, following a telephone call informing them that a forty-one-year-old woman had been shot and had sustained severe head injuries.

As quickly as possible, I was wheeled into the neurosurgical ward that would become my home and my hell for the next three months.

Dr Le Feuvre could clearly see the enormous lacerations to my head as he studied the results of the computerised axial tomography – better known as a CAT scan – that had been done in the trauma unit. The medical team had to assess the damage to my skull, as well as the extent of bruising to and bleeding of the brain. Most importantly, they had to understand the direct impact on the three injured areas of the brain. In medical terms, I had sustained compound depressed skull fractures, a life-threatening condition.

The 'compound' part meant that I had open wounds and that parts of my brain were exposed. It had effectively burst on impact, spilling particles into the wound and allowing others to escape into my bloodied hair and the surface I'd been lying on. The 'depressed' part referred to the fact that bone segments had shifted down from the normal table or skull vault or bed. In layman's terms, my skull had dented inwards when it broke, driving splinters into my brain.

The impact of the blows and subsequent bleeding had also caused severe contusions or bruises to the brain. The mousse-like brain tissue does not tolerate being 'moved' and, in reality, cannot compress and decompress without damage.

In addition, the dura – one of the brain linings that acts as a shield against infection – had been breached, thus heightening the threat of meningitis or other potentially deadly conditions. For Dr Le Feuvre, the first priority was to repair the dura so that I was given the very best chance of warding off secondary infections.

The contusions ranged from mild, soft bruises to haematomas or severe bruises, which carry the risk of excessive bleeding and blood clots.

The surgical team removed as much of the shattered bone as possible, millimetre by millimetre, an extremely delicate and time-consuming procedure. Only then could Dr Le Feuvre turn his attention to the badly lacerated dura. He cleaned it as best he could, then joined the membrane together. His preference was to let the major contusions – which cause swelling and increase pressure on the brain – heal on their own. The alternative was to suck the damaged tissue out, thus decreasing pressure, but that procedure carries the danger of healthy brain tissue being removed as well. He explained to me later that no specialist can accurately predict whether or not injured tissue will heal. It always comes down to the individual physician's judgement, and he opted to treat the contusions conservatively. The fact that I am still able to think and reason is proof that he made the right decision, so thank you, Dr Le Feuvre!

Some of the larger haematomas would thus decompress spontaneously. In other cases, the brain lining was penetrated, the contusion found and the damaged tissue sucked out with a tiny surgical instrument.

Following the surgery, the biggest risk was infection. If that could be staved off, there would still remain the crucial question of underlying damage. That would become apparent only when – and if – I came out of my coma.

The brain is extraordinarily delicate. It has no glucose store and runs out of energy very quickly. Severe and permanent damage can occur within four minutes of diminished blood supply to the brain. Once the primary injuries had been dealt with, the threat of secondary injury remained. A drastic fall in blood pressure due to fresh bleeding or disruption of the brain's oxygen supply as a result of respiratory failure could undo all the painstaking repairs carried out by Dr Le Feuvre and his team. I was also at risk of seizures due to disturbance of the electrolytes or chemicals on which the brain relies to function normally.

It would be a long time before I could fully appreciate the excellence of the care I received. Many months later, when I paid a courtesy call on Dr Le Feuvre, he admitted that he had not given me much chance of survival when he first examined me, and suspected that if I did somehow manage to stay alive, I would be severely impaired.

I was comatose for three weeks. In retrospect, I view that period as a blessing from God. Apparently the brain works in such a way that, when deep injury occurs, it shuts down all high-level functions – sight, hearing, ability to respond – as if it understands that whatever trauma has been suffered is too enormous to deal with in a conscious state. All available energy is then directed at those functions that are needed just to sustain life.

Even after I woke up, it took a long time to understand where I was. I suffered retrograde amnesia, a form of memory loss that is typical of severe trauma, with my short-term memory, concentration, moods and sleeping pattern being restored over a lengthy period of time. Physically, it was the left side of my body that sustained loss of motor function, which means that some parts of my body don't work as well as they once did.

However, I was both incredibly lucky and fortunate to have such excellent care. The consequences of Tony's attack could have been infinitely worse.

Am I the same person that I was? How could I be, after suffering both extensive physical injury and the deepest emotional trauma imaginable? My body and my heart will always bear the scars of my ordeal, but my soul remains intact, my spirit strong.

10

Awakenings

K AREN'S PREMATURE DEATH HAD MADE ME ACUTELY aware of how life could change in the blink of an eye. Even so, nothing could possibly have prepared me for the dire and irreversible consequences of my husband's actions on 16 January 2002.

Three years later, I had embarked on another life-changing experience, but this time, hopefully, the result would bring me joy.

I had already been through two failed attempts to conceive a child by artificial insemination. Both times I had gone through the process of identifying a donor, prepared my parents and myself for the desired outcome, and waited for news with a combination of expectation and fear. After both procedures I had gone home to rest and concentrated on lying as still as I could, my feet up in the air.

Both times, my hopes were dashed within days, and I had to debate afresh my decision to have another child. The doubts and questions never altered: Should I be doing this? What should I do? Should I try again? Why do I want a baby so much? Where are my children? Why has this happened? Am I too old to have another child? How difficult will it be to do this on my own?

For months I rode an emotional roller coaster that drained

me and sent my spirit surging by turn. But in the end, no matter how I phrased the questions, the answer came out the same. I was forty-three years old and my biological clock was running down, but more than anything on earth, I wanted to carry and give birth to another baby – so I had to find a way.

I was advised that my best option would be an embryo implant, using both sperm and an egg from anonymous donors. I had already come to terms with the notion that an unknown stranger would 'father' my child. Now I had to make peace with the fact that the child I longed to have would carry none of my DNA, inherit nothing of my genetic make-up. But he or she would grow in my womb for nine months, come from my body and be mine to raise and nurture, and that would be enough.

In-vitro fertilisation is no quick fix for infertility. It is a delicate procedure that entails weeks – even months – of preparation, tests and screening, yet ultimately all comes down to timing. First, I was put on a course of estrogen tablets to thicken the lining of my uterus. In addition, every day for several weeks I made my way to a clinic for hormone injections. Success would depend on a combination of science and serendipity, on my menstrual cycle matching that of a suitable egg donor, and the doctors knowing just when the moment was right. I watched the calendar like a hawk.

Both sperm and egg donors are screened extensively and, before being accepted, must undergo blood and psychological tests, as well as answer screeds of questions about their medical history, lifestyle and reasons for giving people the chance to be parents. All of this takes time. The sperm donation is the simplest. Once frozen, sperm can be stored for several years before use. The eggs are a different story.

A donor has to have a series of twelve injections, one a day, before her eggs are removed during a surgical procedure. Interestingly, although egg donors are paid a small amount, most are motivated by pure altruism and a genuine desire to help other women know the joy of motherhood. These wonderful and generous people are few and far between, however, and the demand for eggs invariably outstrips the supply.

The normal preparation period for an embryo implant is eight weeks. I had done everything I was supposed to do – had taken all the tests and passed the screening process, had had the injections and pills, eaten healthily, exercised moderately and rested a lot – and now, at last, I was lying on an examination table in Dr Paul le Roux's rooms, staring at the ceiling.

Three days earlier, a medical team had harvested the donor's egg cells, 'washed' them clean of extraneous biological material, injected them with strong, healthy sperm and placed them in an incubator. Within twenty-four hours, the cells had started dividing to form embryos. By the third day it was evident that the embryos were viable and developing strongly, and my doctor notified me that the implant could proceed.

As two of the embryos were gently inserted in my uterus via a microscopic instrument, I thought about the day that Karen had died, the three children I had lost, the way we are transported from the known to the unknown, from the familiar to turmoil, in an instant. I became quite emotional as I acknowledged that this might well be such a moment.

I thought how happy my parents would be for me if the

Mom, Interrupted

procedure worked. We had discussed my plan at length and I had their full support. They had suffered greatly, not only because they had lost three much-loved grandchildren, but also during my recovery and rehabilitation. I could only imagine their anguish when they had first learned our fate and their suffering in the months that followed.

My mother had actually heard a radio news report: '... in Cape Town ... members of a family shot and killed ... three children dead ... mother fighting for her life'. The references to Cape Town and three children caught her ear. The newsreader said the family had lived in Muizenberg, and my mom tried to picture in her mind where the turn-off to Muizenberg was in relation to our house. She said nothing to anyone, but somewhere deep inside, she hoped that we were safe.

She was gardening when my brother Nigel and his wife Jacqui arrived unannounced at about 4 p.m. Both my parents said afterwards that they could see immediately from their faces that something was terribly wrong.

'Nigel, don't tell me this is about the murders in Cape Town,' my mother said anxiously.

'Yes,' he replied, 'it is. Debbie is fighting for her life in hospital. Tony and the kids are dead. They've all been shot.'

Bruce and Tessa arrived soon afterwards. They were all in shock and no one knew what to do next. There were tears and then silence, devastating anger followed by so many questions. Tears rolled down my father's cheeks as he sat, not saying a word, in his favourite chair. My mother couldn't stop crying, shaking her head and walking out of the room, perhaps hoping that when she came back, she would find it had all been a horrible dream. Nigel shared the facts that Inspector Reyneveld had given him when he telephoned. Bruce turned pale and turned to leave the room. The door had slammed shut and he beat his fists against it, cracking and splintering the wood before yanking the door open and running outside.

The last flight of the day from Durban to Cape Town was about to depart. There was no way they could get to the airport in time. Seats for my parents were booked on the first flight in the morning, while my brothers drove to Cape Town, setting out at midnight and arriving at Groote Schuur late in the afternoon the next day.

Months later, my mother told me of her agony as she walked down the hospital corridor to my ward. She knew that Tony and the children were dead and that they had died violently, but she didn't know what I had been through. The doctors had told my parents that my condition was critical and that they should prepare themselves for the possibility that I might not make it. Mom looked down at her feet the whole time, deliberately lagging behind the rest of the group. As panic-stricken as she was about what she would find, she was even more fearful that she was going to be shown my body and told that they had come too late.

As my father entered my room, he could not help himself. 'Oh, my God! Oh, my God!' he wailed. His words forced my mother to look. My father burst into tears. What they saw shocked them to the core. My mother could not even recognise the person in the bed.

My long hair – it had never been short in my life – had been shaved off, except for a few strands hanging oddly from the back of my head to my shoulders. I was hooked up to various monitors and a variety of pipes and drips and drains. My face was swollen out of all proportion and had turned blue around my eyes. I was unconscious.

When Nigel arrived, he sat next to my bed, took my hand and said: 'Debbie, if you can hear me, squeeze my hand.' He repeated this over and over, and apparently I finally did squeeze his hand, but whether that was because I somehow heard and responded to him, or because it was just an involuntary reflex, we don't know.

In consultation with the medical staff, my family agreed that, when they were in my ward, they would say nothing about my condition, what had happened or the fact that Tony and the children were dead, in case I could hear them. There were fleeting moments of consciousness when I became aware that they were with me.

One of the first things my parents did was call Isobel, my childhood friend whose parents still lived across the street in Amanzimtoti. Married now and a highly qualified intensive-care nurse, she was living in Cape Town, but attending a training course in Johannesburg at the time. My father asked her to speak to her colleagues at Groote Schuur and give him a full report on my condition and prognosis, however grave, because he was not convinced that the doctors were telling him the full story. Isobel did as he asked, but while she was able to reassure my parents that I was receiving the best treatment available, she could only confirm what they already knew: my chances of survival were slim and, if I lived, I would more than likely have permanent brain damage.

Awakenings

It fell to my poor parents to deal with the aftermath of what had happened. They had to hear the horrific details from Inspector Reyneveld and learn that Tony was believed to be responsible. They also had to go to the mortuary to identify the children. The first form given to my father to sign was Tony's death certificate. My mother held his hand to try to steady it, but he told the assistant to take the form away. He would not sign it – not then, not ever.

My parents also had to sort out the awful detritus at our house. They packed the children's clothes in boxes and had all the damaged, burned and bloodstained items removed. They had the house cleaned and supervised the repairs. Ironically, Bill Rawson, Tony's business associate, arranged for the furniture to be stored in the vacant Kenilworth house that I had expected we would move to.

One of the hardest decisions my parents and brothers faced concerned a memorial service for the children. I was comatose, and it made no sense to wait until I recovered, since no one knew when or even if that would happen. John Miller, pastor at the church that Katelyn had loved to attend, offered his help, and on 29 January a service was held at His People's Church in N1 City.

In addition to family, friends, teachers and pupils who had known my children, Tony's mother, already in her mid-seventies, and his sister Shelagh were in the packed church. His other sisters, Penny and Jane, were living abroad and couldn't make it.

I was later told that my mother-in-law had come to see me in hospital while I was still in a coma. She subsequently went to live in Australia with Jane. I am still in touch with the family through Penny and Shelagh, and I remain of the opinion that they have suffered greatly, too.

It must have been a lovely service. John opened by reading a message from the families: 'The loss of the children has been a traumatic blow to all the family members and to all of their friends. But the response from people all over the country has been simply overwhelming. Messages of love and support and offers of help pour in every day. It has restored our faith in people, and without their help we would simply not have been able to carry on.'

He prayed for my recovery and that everyone directly touched by the tragedy would find the strength to carry on. Then a large group of children sang the age-old Sunday school hymn, 'All things bright and beautiful'. As their angelic voices faded, John read extracts from the many messages and letters of condolence people had sent. He called them 'love testimonies' that reflected the spirit, character and unique nature of each of my children.

'Kevin was twelve years old and enjoyed school and all his activities. His red hair and pale skin made him conspicuous, and he had to be careful of the sun. He enjoyed the beach and outdoor activities and had many friends. He loved to stay overnight. Like all kids, his manners while at the home of friends were always very good. He was a cheerful and spontaneous child, with a beautiful, sunny disposition. Always willing and helpful, he encapsulated the very essence of a child: a zest for life. He was easily identifiable, with a mischievous twinkle in the eye and an infectious grin on his face. His enthusiastic greetings at school and his ever-present positive attitude made him a delight to teach. He embraced life wholeheartedly and lived each day to the full. Kevin beat his own drum. He had boundless energy and will be sorely missed by all.

'Ten-year-old Katelyn was the most academic of the three children. She excelled at school and at mathematics. She was the accountant of the Redham canteen, and counted the money that her mother had made each day. She loved reading and spent hours with her nose in a book, and she also enjoyed dancing and sports. With blue eyes and platinum-blonde hair, she tanned easily and loved the beach. She had an artistic ability and enjoyed working with clay, paint and watercolours. Never a rowdy child, she could hold her own against her brothers. Katelyn always had a sunny smile and was a kind, happy and friendly girl. She was also shy, gentle and caring, and laughter was always there when she was around. Katelyn looked like her mom. She was a great friend and always shared things. One of her teachers gave thanks for having known Katelyn, calling her a beautiful girl with a delightful smile. This teacher said she saw all the pupils in her class as a garden of flowers, and that Katelyn had blossomed and grown into a generous full bloom that just kept on giving love.

'Nine-year-old Craig was the most gregarious of the three. He learned at an early age how to raise his voice and give his opinion, competing to be heard over his older brother and sister. He enjoyed singing to himself. He was a happy and good-looking child who liked chatting and spoke easily to all, even adults. He made many friends and always helped his mother around the house. Craig loved going to his best friend's house on what he called "adventures" and jumping on the trampoline. They also liked to go fishing together. Craig was loving, caring and affectionate. He made silly jokes to cheer people up and always had a joke up his sleeve. He was a special boy.'

John's sermon was based on God's love for children.

'God has a very special and prominent place for children in his heart. He adores children. It is because of their wonderful simplicity and faith, their wonderful love. In many ways it is because of their deep understanding of life. Today, we need to understand that it is God's grace, love and mercy that we have to receive. It is almost impossible to deal with the tragedy that has unfolded. Death means an end of time on earth. It is a time of separation between our bodies and our spirits.

'God loved these children and he loves us. He wants to pass on some of his characteristics to us. I think God is love and he is the father of love. Love of God is manifested through us. God loved us first. On this sad day, we need to receive his love. We need each drop. His love is here – it will take away the hurt, pain and suffering. We can lean on God, we can trust him. In our deepest moments of sorrow, we must remember the inner joy that God holds for each of us.

'Yes, we are struggling with sadness. But we must not have troubled hearts. In the moment of death for Kevin, Katelyn and Craig, God was there to receive them. He went before them, he received them and he loves them. He is protecting them, he understands them and he is with them now. In real time. Heaven is a real place. When we know God, death no longer has its sting.'

The congregation sang a hymn of thanks for the lives of my

three children – *I will lift my eyes to the hills. My help cometh from the Lord, all of my help cometh from the Lord* – and then John said a final prayer:

'God, as we sit here, we have a hole in our hearts. It is shaped in your image. Come in, become my Lord, saviour, king and friend. Thank you, Jesus, for saving me. Lord, as we commit these three precious children to the grave, the dust returns to the earth as it was. The spirit has already gone to God who gave it. Amen.'

The service ended with the lovely hymn, 'Shine, Jesus, Shine'. The words are beautiful:

>Shine, Jesus, shine,
>Fill this land
>With the father's glory!
>Blaze, spirit, blaze,
>Set our hearts on fire!
>Flow, river flow,
>Fill the nations with grace and mercy,
>Send forth your word!
>More than all
>Let there be love!

For me, the most inspiring part of John's service were the words: 'What is death? It is a coming home, a divine welcome to well-loved children.' They gave me something to believe in when I had lost faith in all else.

Of course, at the time he read those words, I was lying unconscious in a hospital bed. It would be another two weeks before my wounded brain began flickering back to life. There were moments when I realised I was waking up, when I had a sense that something had happened, but I still couldn't comprehend what. From time to time, I became aware that my parents and brothers were near my bed. Mostly, though, I felt confused, uneasy. Sometimes there was absolute dread and horror, at others a strange sensation of peace, a feeling that I could just let go and drift off into nothingness.

The media reported that I was fighting for my life, and they were right. For a long time, I teetered on the brink of death. I don't know what ultimately made the pendulum swing in favour of life, but I believe it was the thought of my children that kept me alive. In the haze of confusion, I seemed to have forgotten everything – including my own name – except that I was the mother of Kevin, Katelyn and Craig. No matter what had happened, I knew I had to break through the barriers that were keeping us apart, that I had to find my children, whatever that took.

I was still being heavily sedated to prevent seizures, yet there was one morning when I *knew* I was waking up, but that something was terribly wrong. I became aware that I was lying in a bed and was in pain as the result of something that had happened. A car accident? Was I in trouble? Where were the kids? Was Hazel with them? Why couldn't I hear her? And where was Tony?

Suddenly, I felt a violent anger towards my husband. Why hadn't he brought the children to me? Why wasn't he here with me? Was he late?

That was when I heard Kevin's cries, frightened, desperate. *Mommy! Mommy! Mommy!*

Oh, thank God, I thought, he's here! Katelyn and Craig

must be with him. But why did he sound so scared? I struggled to sit up, driven now to find the children. I saw the doctors come into the room and stand by my bed. Good, I thought, they can help me find Hazel and the kids. But they stared at me in silence, and I thumped the mattress with my fist in anger and frustration.

It was at that moment, Dr Le Feuvre said, that he knew the time had come for me to learn the brutal truth. He had no idea how I would react and would have preferred to wait, but it was obvious that I was in mental torment, and this was causing me undue physical distress as well.

When my parents arrived at the hospital to visit, he advised them of his decision. They had been terrified that one of them would have to break the news. Not only were they still trying to come to terms with the loss of their grandchildren, they were also consumed with anxiety about me. They came into my room with Dr Le Feuvre and all three of them found a place to sit next to me on the bed.

'Debbie,' the doctor said gently, 'do you know why you are here?' I looked at him and shook my head. 'Do you have any idea why you are here?' I shook my head again.

'Debbie, you're here in the hospital because you've been severely assaulted by your husband. You sustained very serious injuries to your head,' he said.

I remember feeling somewhat disinterested. My only and immediate need was to find out where my children were, and so I asked him. I don't believe I ever expected to hear him say: 'Your children are dead. Your husband also did not survive.'

Anger coursed through my veins, and somehow I knew

it was directed at Tony. What had he done? What had he done to my children?

My mother told me later that I simply stared at Dr Le Feuvre blankly, tears rolling down my face. I cried without saying a word. I have no recollection of that. In my mind, I was shrieking and screaming and it felt as if something had ripped my insides out, exposing every raw nerve in my body.

Over the next few days, I was told the main details, in small doses. I had to hear that Tony had injured me so badly that I might not recover completely. I had to hear that the children were bludgeoned with an axe as they lay sleeping in their beds. I had to hear that Tony had shot himself. My mom cried as she told me they had already held a memorial service for the children.

It is not possible to describe the excruciating pain, distress and helplessness I went through as the irrevocable reality of my loss sank in. It would be almost two years before I could muster the courage to enter a church again, and at least that long before I found a patch of solid ground, a base strong enough for me to let go of my children and of the person I had been for so much of my adult life – Debbie, wife of Tony and mother of three.

11

Finding my feet

FOR THE FIRST FEW WEEKS FOLLOWING MY ADMISSION to Groote Schuur, I was obviously – and thankfully – heavily sedated. After that, the nursing staff would ask me every evening if I wanted something for the pain or to help me sleep, but as time passed, all my medication was reduced.

I had always been wary of pills and potions, but now I felt like swallowing everything that was available to take the pain away, especially the emotional anguish. Fortunately, however, from somewhere deep inside, I found the resilience to refuse most of what was offered. I really do believe this helped me in the long run. Somehow, suffering rather than suppressing the pain contributed to the healing. If I had become dependent on pills at that time, I would have merely postponed the inevitable. At some point or another, I would have had to confront not only my emotions, but possibly an addiction as well. I am grateful to have been spared that ordeal, but I understand only too well how easily it might happen.

As my awareness increased and I could feel most parts of my body, the depressing realisation dawned that my left side was paralysed. Suddenly, I had to deal with the devastating thought that I was physically damaged beyond repair. My injuries were permanent and would have a severe impact on my life. I was disabled, and it seemed I would have to rely on others to help me perform even the most basic functions in future. My independence, my life as I had known it, had moved beyond my reach.

My friend Shaun had visited me in hospital when I was in a coma. He would sit on the side of the bed, hold my hand and admonish me gently: 'Girl, you've got a lot of explaining to do! There are obviously a whole lot of things you have not told us. You have to wake up and do some explaining.'

Now, as I saw his face peeping around the door and he walked towards my bed, I was grateful for the distraction and the positive aura that seemed to surround him.

'Oh no, Debbie! Really, I simply cannot stand it any more. The hair must go. These long strings of fluff down your back simply make me manic! They have to go! You are lucky that you won't have to wait till you turn fifty to cut your hair short! And the anaesthesia has done nothing for the colour. Sit up, doll!'

With that, he pulled a black hairdressing cape from his shoulder bag, along with brushes, clippers and everything else he needed. I was still struggling to form the words 'but' and 'is it safe' and 'ask the nurse', but the clipper was already plugged in.

There was a sense of safety in letting go, just giving over. Beyond a dull and aching numbness, that was all I felt as I managed to say: 'Shaun, he took my children. I am so scared that I will never feel again …'

'Darling, yes, he took your children, he maimed you, but you know what? The best thing you can do is fight back – for the kids. *You* have to live for *them*. You have got to put your

Finding my feet

lipstick on! Without the lipstick you can't have a positive attitude! You have to learn to think positive, act positive, feel positive. Sit up, doll, here's some lipliner. Come now, you can't be seen without war paint on! Let's colour them lips!

'You simply ruined my birthday! There I was, expecting a simply delicious day, only to hear on the news that you'd been clobbered over the head! You can't do that to me on my birthday! Spoiled it all, you did!'

In the beginning, his banter was just words that washed over me, but it put me at ease. I felt better when Shaun was there, as if my burden was lighter, and for a short while all that mattered was to laugh and have fun.

My hospital-assigned physiotherapist, Frankie, was a powerfully built young man whose passion for his work allowed no laziness. He arrived each day like clockwork, parking that awful wheelchair next to my bed, lifting me into it and pushing me to the rehabilitation centre. I came to think of the hard exercise bed as Frankie's torture chamber.

Weeks of confinement to bed had taken a toll on my muscles. My normal weight of 50 kilograms had fallen to 35 kilograms, and every physical movement was painful and exhausting. It has to be said that Frankie was almost certainly a bit of a sadist, though. No matter how piteously I begged for a rest or massage, he refused, insisting that I put more effort into the exercises. I was used to being fit and strong. I'd danced for a long time and spent many hours at the gym, but now my body seemed to have forsaken me. Even the simplest exercises left me sweating and exhausted.

Physiotherapy became as much a mental as a physical

challenge. I developed a mantra that I would recite silently through every session: 'I *will* get up and walk out of this hospital. I *will* do this for myself and for my children. I will not rest until it is done.' I convinced myself that Kevin, Katelyn and Craig would never find peace if their father's actions left me so disabled that I would spend the rest of my life in a wheelchair or trapped in a small room, dependent on others for my every need. I became obsessed with the idea of being healed, dedicating every set of exercises to one of my children: 'This one is for you, Kevin' (or Katelyn, or Craig).

Then Shaun's face would come to mind and I'd hear him urging me on: 'I know you don't feel like looking good or getting strong, but you simply have no choice. I have a salon to run. I can't come here year in and year out. Only the people from *The Bold and the Beautiful* look good in bed. You simply have to go on. Work those muscles, girlie, work them!

'You say there's nothing to live for, but that's not true. What about Hazel? She's waiting for you to come and fetch her. We'll have to make sure you wear a wig when you pick her up. Where's that hairpiece that you used to wear? Oh, I suppose it went up in flames with the rest of your past. You see, darling, everything is new! You have a whole new life to live! How many people get that chance? A whole new beginning! It's just marvellous! Come on, lift that chin ... think of Hazel.'

I'd do the next set for my wonderful and supportive friends and follow it with a set for all the people who didn't even know me, but had sent good thoughts and wishes and prayers.

One morning about two months after I'd awakened, a young man was just getting to his feet as Frankie wheeled me into the

Finding my feet

physio room. I gauged from the staff's reaction that this was the first time he had been able to stand on his own. I realised how hard he must have worked to reach that point, and was inspired, for the first time, by the possibility that I, too, would be able to stand up again. I said nothing as Frankie put me through my usual half-hour routine, then took me back to my room where I could fall into a deep, exhausted sleep.

About a week later, the young man still very much on my mind, I asked Frankie: 'Do *you* think I can stand?' He replied: 'Do you think you can stand?'

I said: 'Frankie, I *will* stand!'

So I sat on the edge of the bed with my feet flat on the floor. Frankie kneeled down in front of me and said, 'Debbie, when you're ready, move your weight onto both feet and see if you can hold it there for a while.'

I sat there gathering my strength and telling myself: 'Debbie, you will stand. You will stand! You will get up – for your children, for your friends, for yourself. And you will stand up for Tony, to ensure that what remains are memories of the happy times we had, not the disability the assault caused. The better you recover, the less the damage that was done. You will stand!'

I rocked to and fro a couple of times, then pushed my body forward – and suddenly found myself upright! Frankie grabbed me around the waist to support my fragile frame and, as I straightened my back, he shouted at the other therapist: 'Liza, Liza! Look, Debbie is standing!' He was over the moon and Liza cheered.

Then Frankie said: 'Debbie, do you think you can take a few steps?'

I said: 'Frankie, I will take a few steps.'

He held me lightly as I manoeuvred my feet into position. It felt utterly strange. My mind remembered how to walk, but somehow my body had forgotten. Then I took my first, hesitant step. Frankie and Liza could barely contain their excitement, and I was overwhelmed.

When he took me back to my room, Frankie rang the bell frantically to call the nurses. He parked the wheelchair about ten paces from the bed and, before I could offer any resistance, helped me up, supported my back and locked one of his arms around one of mine. 'Watch this! Come one Debbie, let's show them,' he said triumphantly.

To their amazement – and my own – I walked to the bed. With each step the cheers got louder, and by the time I collapsed on the bed, it was a riot. It felt as if I had just run a marathon. Someone fetched a cold drink from the fridge as a reward. I just lay there trying to recover, and a short while later my parents arrived.

My mom fed me some yoghurt and then, still feeling drained and thirsty, I had another cold drink. My parents left soon afterwards, and they could not even have reached the exit before I was ringing for help. When a nurse came, I said I needed to go to the toilet, lifted myself up and swung my legs off the bed. Now that I knew I could walk, there was no way I was going to use a bedpan!

I walked to the toilet, telling the nurse: 'Don't you ever bring that pan into my room again! I never want to see it again!' As I reached the bathroom door, everything started spinning. 'Bring the pan, I'm going to be sick!' I yelled, just before collapsing in a heap on the floor. The yoghurt and cold drinks all came up. The excitement had proved just too much, but I will never forget how it felt to stand on my own two feet again. It was a momentous signal that I could break free of the horror in which I'd been trapped for months. Tony would *not* condemn me to a wheelchair for the rest of my days. I had found the escape hatch, and the 'prison' he'd sentenced me to would not hold me forever.

Once I knew that I could walk again, other possibilities arose. Perhaps I could learn to use my left arm again. Perhaps, one day, I might even be able to feel joy again. Needless to say, euphoria made way for reality soon enough.

Early mornings were the worst times, though darkness held its own pernicious terror. I would wake up in a confused haze, thinking I was in my own bed at home, only to remember and go through the whole process again of losing my children, my husband, Hazel and my former life, day after day. Things that I had made peace with the day before would have to be confronted anew, until I screamed out loud in anger, pain and frustration. By the time the doctors made their first rounds, I was usually in tears.

The nights were frightful. I slept fitfully, my mind churning with unanswered questions, but, in addition, I had become quite paranoid. At times I was utterly convinced that Tony must have been involved in some or other sinister deal and that a bloodthirsty gang had attacked us. I was certain that on hearing I had survived, they would come and finish me off. I would lie in bed shivering with fear, convinced that every sound was a killer coming into my room.

My mother would try to comfort me. 'Debbie, you are six floors up, no one can get to you. No one is after you.'

How could she know that? A few months ago, I had had no inkling that my children and I were in any danger. I rang the bell next to my bed incessantly, seeking reassurance from the nurses. Why is there a light on? Who walked past the door? What was that noise?

A trauma counsellor came to see me on Tuesdays and Thursdays and helped relieve some of my anxieties, but it must have been incredibly difficult for the staff at Groote Schuur to cope with my fears and demands. To their credit, they never showed impatience or made me feel uncomfortable. Bless them.

I was really battling to accept my situation. Along with the many questions, I felt enormous guilt that my children had died and I had not. What had they done for their lives to end so horribly? What had I contributed to their deaths? What could I have done differently? How could I have avoided this? Why, why, why?

There was never a moment that I didn't long for them, for Hazel, and also for Tony. My feelings about him were the source of some of my greatest confusion. There was an almighty anger, ranging from red-hot to icy – resentment, blame, even hatred – yet I still loved him. Although there had been times of great unhappiness in our marriage, a part of me had always loved Tony, for better or for worse. My towering rage against him stood in strange contradiction to my genuine sadness at losing him and still feeling love for him. Occasionally, in my more rational moments, I thought about forgiving him. I argued that he must have been in unfathomable turmoil to do what he did. He must have wrestled a beast inside him before giving up the fight. Often I would struggle intensely with the demon of guilt. Had I had a share in my children's death? But in such moments I had to cling to the knowledge that the decision he'd taken had been his alone. I would take responsibility for my share of the problems in our marriage, the shortcomings in our relationship, but nothing I'd done or lacked, however hurtful or important, could ever have justified his final act.

The decision to take the lives of his children, leave their mother for dead and kill himself was Tony's, and he alone must bear the culpability.

12

Starting over

AFTER THREE MONTHS AT GROOTE SCHUUR, I WAS transferred to the Conradie Care Centre in Pinelands, about ten kilometres away. Dr Le Feuvre believed that I was well on the road to recovery, but would benefit from the specialised physical and occupational therapy offered there.

My injuries had healed to the point where they no longer required medical attention. Only the scars remained. The next step was to deal with the non-visible damage and reprogramme my brain to find new pathways to restore my movements and fine motor functions. While there were no guarantees, there was hope. Dr Le Feuvre was happy with the progress I had made and told me that further improvement could be expected over the next eighteen months. In cases of severe brain injury such as mine, he said, it could easily take up to two years for the body to heal. Only then would I reach the point beyond which no more recovery would be likely.

I was in that small room at Groote Schuur for a long time, and by the time I left, I had most of my fears under control. But there was still a deep underlying sense of anxiety and distrust. There had been times when I hated that room, when I was desperate to go home; now I was afraid to leave the familiar faces and what had been my little world for months. Throughout my time at Groote Schuur, I left that room only

Mom, Interrupted

to go to other parts of the hospital for tests and physiotherapy, or for short walks down the corridor. I had not been outside at all.

When the time came to leave, I came undone. I cried and begged to stay, but to no avail. The ambulance was waiting. It was very hard to say goodbye to everyone who had taken care of me.

Lying in the back of the ambulance, I felt abandoned and vulnerable. The woman attendant accompanying me must have sensed my distress and she started talking to me. Unfortunately, she chose to share her memories of the 'horrible incident' at my home. This was the first time I'd heard someone other than family, friends and caregivers talk about what had happened. On the one hand, her account terrified me. On the other, I had a morbid need to listen to her. What if she knew something that no one else had told me? All along, I had insisted on hearing all the details, however ghastly, believing that the more I knew, the fewer questions would be left unanswered.

She'd heard the calls from the emergency personnel to their base on the ambulance radio while on the way to Fish Hoek to fetch a patient. While waiting for the traffic lights to change, she said, the van taking the bodies of my husband and children to the Salt River mortuary had driven through the intersection, right in front of her.

Something in me shattered. I could not bear to think of strangers picking up my children's charred remains and placing them in black plastic body bags to be transported to a cold, sterile place. That image played out in my head, over and over, all the way to Conradie. God! It was absolutely awful.

Starting over

As if I wasn't already distressed enough, the driver pulled up at the men's section of the centre! I was already in the foyer when someone realised the mistake and I was promptly pushed back into the ambulance. This time, they delivered me to the children's wing.

When at last I was admitted to the women's section, I was assigned to share a room with a recovering alcoholic and drug addict. She was obviously fighting her own demons, and this unsettled me even more. I pleaded to be taken back to Groote Schuur, which was out of the question, of course, but at least they moved me to a private room. What a first day out!

As I unpacked my belongings, I was tearful and angry. The reality of my loneliness had finally dawned on me. How was I going to start a new life? All the possible scenarios I had thought about so far were impossible dreams. I was alone and empty, and I had no idea how to start building a new life. What did that mean? I didn't even *want* a 'new' life. I wanted my old life back.

Yet again, I wondered if it would not have been better to have died. Perhaps it still would. Even the skies outside were grey and miserable. Death was so inviting ... death made sense. Surely death would still the longing, end the pain?

The cherished faces of my children swam before my eyes. Then I saw my parents and brothers, all the friends who had offered me their love and support, and, finally, Karen, begging, pleading, negotiating for just one more month or week or day to live.

It took years for me to understand how perilously close I had come to a complete breakdown as 2002 rolled inexorably on. At times, my close friends were my only connection to sanity. I would sit on my bed or in a wheelchair and watch the door for a face I recognised, convinced in my own mind that I had gone over the edge, that I was hopelessly mad, damaged goods condemned to eternal loneliness. Then a familiar face would appear, someone would say cheerfully, 'Hello, Debbie!' and pull me back from the brink.

At Conradie, my routine consisted of going from bed to the bathroom or physiotherapy and back. The one face I did not look forward to seeing was that of Tasneem, the physiotherapist who had taken over where Frankie left off, but every morning at nine, there he was, grinning broadly as he poked his head around my door. He was Mr Hell. He would push the wheelchair up to the side of my bed and urge me cheerily, 'Come on, hop on!' He was like a strident alarm clock. Like Frankie, Tasneem prided himself on being an 'aggressive' therapist, and the only way to meet the challenges he dished out was to surrender and just do the damn exercises. There were times when I was convinced that I was doing more harm than good – nothing that felt so bad could be good for you, I reasoned – but I was not going to give him the satisfaction of quitting, so our love–hate relationship continued.

Sometimes, my anger at Tony provided enough fuel to get me through a gruelling session. Others still ended in tears, but for the most part, it was the support of friends and caring people with the hearts of angels that impelled me to go on.

They would come and talk to me, sit with me, offer help, advice, money, practical assistance, not once but many times. I will never be able to thank them enough, but they should know

Starting over

that, at a time when I was deeply needy, suspicious of all people and their motives, uncertain about what I felt and for whom, their love and countless acts of caring built a bridge from total despair to tolerable pain. When my own emotional reserves were utterly depleted, my friends lent me some of theirs, gave me a reason to get well and go on living.

Liz, Kelly and Isobel came twice a week to help me bath. Isobel was a special pillar of strength and, best of all, she made me laugh. While she was visiting one day, an orderly came to take me for X-rays. Jokingly, I suggested that Isobel should hide under the bedclothes so that we'd bamboozle the doctors when they were presented with a two-headed scan. She played along, pretending to jump onto the foot of the bed. We were in hysterics.

There were other precious moments. Isobel once asked what I missed most about not being able to scoot around in my car. 'A Magnum ice cream,' I said. The next day she brought me one, smuggled it in and blocked the view from the doorway while I ate it. What simple but delicious pleasure that brought!

My neighbour Peggy (not her real name) helped break the monotony of my days with her bizarre behaviour. She was a real character and, for a short time, my roommate. She was a chain smoker, and for some reason stored all her cigarette butts in the drawer of her nightstand and flicked ash down the front of her dress. I never found out why she was at Conradie, but my impression was that she lived there permanently.

One day, as she passed me in her wheelchair, she suddenly blurted out: 'Are you a lesbian?'

Surprised, I answered, 'No, I'm not. Why do you ask?'

'Well, you all go to the bathroom together. What do the

four of you do there? You must be a lesbian,' she said. After that, whenever she saw me, she would point a finger at me and shout, 'You're a lesbian!' I asked her to stop talking nonsense, but she never did. Eventually, she said it once too often, on a day when I was especially frustrated and irritable. 'Look,' I said, 'if you say that once more, I will slap you.'

My mother rushed out of my room to grab me. 'Debbie, are you mad? Don't threaten her. People will think you've gone nuts! They'll keep you here longer,' she said. I was past caring. I kept saying 'I'll smack her!' It made no difference.

Some time after that, as my trio of 'bathing belles' wheeled me down the corridor to the bathroom, we passed Peggy. She had dropped something on the floor and Liz bent to pick it up. Peggy grabbed her by the shoulder and said, 'Don't touch me, you lesbian!' Liz just laughed. I apologised on Peggy's behalf, but my wonderful friends giggled all the way through my ablutions.

Peggy never bathed. She refused to, and heaven only knows when last she had immersed her fiftysomething body in a tub of water! Before I left Conradie, I did go to say goodbye to her. I was used to her strange ways by then and felt quite sorry for her. I sometimes wonder what has happened to her and if she is till there.

Towards the end of my stay I was allowed to spend weekends 'out'. During all the time I was hospitalised, I never saw a newspaper, but one Saturday morning when my parents came to pick me up, I noticed an old one lying in their car. I turned it over and found myself staring at a half-page photograph of Tony under the headline 'Married to an axe murderer' in big black letters. I was horrified. How dare they portray him as

Starting over

some kind of monster? He was never a monster – was he? Of course not. I'd loved him. He couldn't have been a beast. But he had done a terrible thing ... oh, the turmoil that encounter with the media set off in my mind.

The day after my forty-first birthday on 20 March, I finally got the chance to thank the emergency personnel who had saved my life and the medical staff who had put the broken pieces back together. We invited them to a small party in the garden of friends who lived in Tokai, and I was able to tell the firemen, paramedics, helicopter crew, doctors, nurses and therapists how grateful I was for their help. This was my first 'public' appearance since the attack and it helped prepare me for an even bigger gathering.

Towards the end of January, some of my friends had suggested to my parents that a trust fund should be set up to cover my medical and other expenses. I had no medical aid and of course no income, and without the generous donations made by friends as well as total strangers, I don't know how we would have coped. The fund was duly started, with my father and brother Nigel as trustees. People opened their hearts and wallets wide, and in addition to direct contributions, friends arranged a golf day and a dance at the Kelvin Grove Club in support of the fund.

The dance also gave me the opportunity to bid farewell to everyone in Cape Town who had sustained my parents and unflinchingly supported me over the most difficult months of our lives. By now, it had become clear that I would have to leave Cape Town and return to live in Amanzimtoti, with my parents. More than 300 people – many of them complete strangers – bought tickets. As the dance approached, I became increasingly nervous. The thought of walking into a packed room and having to speak in front of such a large crowd made me vomit with fear. I had lost so much weight that none of my clothes fitted, I could still not walk unaided, and my left arm dangled uselessly at my side. My hair was just starting to grow back and the scars on my scalp would be a blatant and ugly reminder of why we were there at all.

But I knew I had to do it. The least I could offer the many people who had rallied round us was a personal 'thank you'. Amazingly, when I entered the hall that night, though all eyes were on me, I felt neither awkward nor an object of curiosity. An overwhelming aura of love and kindness seemed to radiate from all those present and wrap me in its welcoming warmth.

My brother Nigel and I had agreed that when I made my little speech, he would stand with me. Should my emotions gain the upper hand, he would deliver the rest of my message for me. I shuffled to the podium and immediately realised that I couldn't make out a word of what I had prepared, because I hadn't brought my reading glasses. So I improvised, calling out the names, one by one, of all the people who had done so much for me while I was in hospital, and asking them to come and stand beside me. These were truly the people, each in his or her inimitable way, who had saved my life – one by massaging my feet, another by giving me a manicure, still others by giving up their time to just sit and chat or, equally important, listen. They were there in my darkest moments and my gratitude was immeasurable.

I couldn't say the words I really wanted them to hear. I had written: 'If Kevin, Katelyn and Craig could be here tonight,

Starting over

they would thank all of you for loving and supporting their mother.' I passed the piece of paper to my brother and he read that message for me.

One of my friends was married to a musician whose band played for us that night. Before the dance, she had asked if there was a special song I wanted them to play. 'Yes,' I joked, 'Gloria Gaynor's "I will survive"!' Now, surrounded by my closest and dearest friends and family, I heard the first notes of the song. It was just the most amazing moment. Everyone in that hall joined in, singing, dancing and starting to show signs that a serious party was in the making.

Part of the evening was devoted to an auction of various donated items. This alone raised R20 000. One family paid R8 000 for a handmade teddy bear, then promptly gave it to me as a gift. I burst into tears. My children had so loved their teddy bears, cuddling them each night as they went to sleep.

All too soon, it seemed, the band announced that they were about to play their last number, after which I would take my leave. Everyone stood up and formed a huge circle around the dance floor. I made my way from one to the other, saying 'thank you' and 'goodbye'. We cried, we hugged, we kissed and comforted one another. I had no way of knowing whether I would ever see these people again or even return to Cape Town. I will never forget that night.

But the only logical thing for me to do was go back to Amanzimtoti and live with my parents. I needed looking after, physically and emotionally, and none of us knew how long that would be the case. But before I could leave, there was something that I had to do. I had thought about it long and hard, but I knew I could not leave the Cape without returning to the house at 19 Cannon Island Way, Marina da Gama, where my children had died.

Pastor John Miller was waiting for us when my father parked in front of the property. Carrying three bunches of roses, I stepped through the front door. The house was empty and being repainted, but, even so, I had not expected that it would feel so unfamiliar, nor I so detached. I traced in reverse the path that Tony had taken as he carried the children to the study, laying a bunch of flowers in each of their bedrooms. In each, as well, I dropped to my knees and prayed: 'Dear God, please forgive! Kevin, I miss you so much. I don't understand. I don't know what to say. I will never forget you. I am here for you.'

I touched the carpet where my children's feet had trod. 'I am sorry that Mommy could not save you. I am sorry about what Daddy had done. I don't know why he did this. I would have done anything to keep you safe, to save you, to be with you. But I could not. I am so, so sorry.

'I know, as you knew, that Daddy loved you and I never thought he would do anything to hurt you. He must have been really sick, but all you have to remember is that he did love you, and I will always love you, wherever you are. We will always be together, a family, and my heart is with you always.'

Then I made my way to the study. As I entered, an uncontrollable anger rose in me. I felt as if I were on the verge of exploding. I dropped to my knees, then fell forward on the floor and screamed: 'Tony, what have you done? What have you done? Why did you do this?'

My father rushed forward and grabbed my arm, but John

Starting over

stopped him. 'Leave her,' he said softly. 'Give her a moment.'

I shouted at Tony again. 'Why? Why did you not tell me? Why did you not talk to me if there was a problem? Why did you not share this!'

I couldn't stop wailing, over and over, 'Tony! Tony, why?'

In the years since then, people have often asked, 'But how do you manage? How did you carry on after what happened?' I have to say that as taxing as some days are, as difficult as my present life can be, I constantly draw strength from my treasured memories. A lot of people care about me, help me and hold me in their hearts and thoughts. When I am sad or depressed, I call up the faces of so many good and true and loving friends, and remind myself how passionately Karen had wanted to stay alive.

I was going to fly to Durban, accompanied by an aunt, Jean Edley. The aircraft took off on a Sunday evening. Walking slowly across the tarmac to board was one of the lowest points of my life. I was lonely, confused and sad beyond words. I was leaving the place I called home. Worst of all, I was leaving my children behind.

I had left my parents' home years before, healthy and filled with hope for the future. I was returning to it disabled and emotionally shattered. I felt betrayed, unsafe and in the grip of naked fear. I found my seat and fastened the belt around my waist. As the aircraft pushed back and prepared for take-off, I stared blankly out of the window and made no effort to hide my tears. I was conscious of a feeling I had never known before and I had no idea how to handle it. It was an all-consuming desolation that no human being should ever have to face.

13

Homeward bound

After only a few days at Amanzimtoti, I was distraught. My frame of reference had become the same ceiling I had stared at as a child. My mind raced day and night with questions and overpowering uncertainty.

I felt trapped, caged. Mental and physical damage had condemned me to being a child again, for the rest of my days. I was bogged down in the present, unable to move forward, incapable of looking back. In desperation, I called the trauma counsellor who had treated me in Cape Town. She recommended that I see Clive Morgan, a psychologist in my area.

I'd never been to a psychologist before, and when my father dropped me at the purple house where Clive had his rooms, I had no idea what to expect. The man who held out a hand of welcome and showed me to a comfortable seat was a gentle, cheerful soul with a healthy sense of humour. He'd been a pilot with the South African Air Force when, as he put it, 'planes were made of string and men of steel'. His interest in psychology was aroused while working for the navy. He was a happily married father of three adult children, and I liked him immediately. His eyes were soft, his gaze gentle. The poor, sweet man had no idea what he was letting himself in for!

Clive's many years of counselling had imbued him with

patience, tolerance and wisdom. It was just as well that he found his work rewarding, as my case was certainly not financially lucrative. I was practically destitute, and he never charged me the full fee, though I insisted on paying what I could.

I'd been told that brain injuries, especially to the frontal lobe, carried the risk of temper tantrums (now I had an excuse!), promiscuity (ditto!) and an inability to work with money (double ditto!). What with my paralysed arm and hand, hideous scars and speech impediment, no wonder Clive's initial assessment was one of severe mental and physical trauma.

For most of our early sessions, I did little except stare at Clive. I didn't know what to say, could not remember certain words, was unable to physically form those that I did recollect and my memory was fragmented. The only thing I kept on asking was, why? Clive later told me that, in the beginning, he had detected little depth of emotion. When I answered his questions, it was as if I was talking about a movie rather than my life. When I showed tears or anger, there was no passion, as if I were a child crying over a misplaced toy.

Clive's first priority was to make me feel at home and relaxed in his presence. He listened to my endless complaints without censure, recommended a mild antidepressant and accepted me unconditionally. Gradually, I began to feel safe with him.

In that early stage of therapy, he considered referring me to a special support group for adults who had suffered severe brain damage as the result of a stroke or accident. The primary objective was to help such people lead a relatively normal life despite being heavily dependent on others. As time passed, however, he began to feel a glimmer of hope that I might make a significant spontaneous recovery. He noticed that my speech was slowly improving, saw glimpses of my aloofness and bluntness lifting, and detected the first indications of real emotion.

For the second time since that dreadful January morning, a health professional eschewed the textbook approach and gambled that his instincts would offer me the best possible chance of recovery. Dr Le Feuvre's conservative treatment of the bruising and bleeding in my brain had unquestionably helped to minimise the permanent physical damage. Now Clive decided that group therapy might not be my best bet, after all. Instead, he would let me lead the way through the uncharted waters of my tormented psyche, trusting that I would grow along the way, while he followed one step behind.

He later admitted that he had had no idea what direction I would take, how long I would need to reach my journey's end or how I would cope with the dangers lurking along the way. He could only trust that he would recognise potential risks in time and be able to reverse out of red-light situations. If not, I might easily slip over the edge and retreat into a psychotic state, or revert to the defensive bluntness that I had adopted as an emotional shield.

At one point, he told me later, he felt that there were far more holes in the dyke than he could plug with his ten fingers, and feared that he was dangerously close to losing me. I think we skirted disaster several times, but something always pulled me back from the brink – Clive himself, a phone call from a friend, a resilience I didn't know I had. I am grateful to Clive for being brave enough to believe in my ability to heal, to vanquish the demons that Tony's actions had visited upon me. If not for his courage, I would more than likely have been shackled to a frustrating, dependent, mentally unstable existence.

The first enemy was my anger. I had become aggressive and deeply resentful, especially towards Tony and my parents. It had been decades since I lived under their roof. They were in their seventies and had been given a somewhat pessimistic prognosis for my condition. Understandably, they were scared and overprotective, watching me closely, uncertain how much I could handle, wary of upsetting me. Born of unadulterated love, their well-intentioned caring served only to heighten my frustration at the time.

Clive agreed that I had reason to be angry, but taught me that I could choose how to act this out. I tried my best, but it was a difficult and challenging time for me and my parents, and I'm afraid I often failed. I spent a great deal of time on the phone. Isobel listened patiently and gave solid, calming advice. Shaun would spend up to an hour at a time talking to me in his inimitable manner.

'Time is the greatest healer. It's all you have, but it will heal you. You have to start living for yourself. Think of what you want. Only Debbie knows what Debbie needs, darling. Work with Clive! Unpack all the old issues and then let's move on to a new beginning. By the way, don't you dare have your hair cut and coloured and then expect me to fix up the mess! Focus on the light at the end of the tunnel. There is someone, something, waiting for you there. Hazel will be there and a new life. Now work that old baggage, darling …'

Clive understood that I needed to assert whatever degree of

independence I could attain. I started seeing a physiotherapist again in order to regain the fullest possible use of my left arm and hand. But, as I ventured deeper into the muddy whirlpool of my emotions, I became increasingly depressed. Each time Clive gently probed the question of my children, I shut down. Knowing that their loss lay at the very core of my deepest sadness, he kept on prodding until, during one session, my eyes filled with tears and he realised that I was finally ready to deal with their deaths.

Over the months that followed, I mourned, I grieved, I wept and wailed as I finally acknowledged the unspeakable pain of losing Kevin, Katelyn and Craig. At times, Clive worried that I would be overwhelmed by the raw emotions that were surfacing. Other times, he was amazed by how much progress I seemed to be making. My memory of that period is confined to intense pain and buckets of tears.

I revisited the house, the trauma, my children's personalities, my feelings about Tony over and over, until I was able to accept, at an intellectual level, that it was all over and would never be again. I began to understand that a deep discontinuity had occurred in my life.

Then the longing came. Longing for their faces, their little hands and bodies, lazy days with them. Longing for Hazel. Longing for Tony. Longing for friends. I was consumed by a yearning to be close to all of it again. I'd been seeing Clive for almost a year when I realised, with utter clarity, that I had to go back to Cape Town. I had heard much about that elusive, indefinable thing called 'closure' and, whatever it was, I knew that I could find it nowhere else. Cape Town was still 'home' and I wanted to go there. I needed to say goodbye to my children, and I could do so only in the place where we had last been together.

My parents, family and friends were vigorous and vocal in their opposition. Who would take care of me? Where would I live? How would I support myself? What if something went wrong?

Clive understood. He helped me draw up a plan of action that would culminate in my return to Cape Town. He believed the 'child' had grown into a young adult and was ready to take charge of her life again. I will always be grateful for his support and practical advice. He enriched, empowered and enabled me. He set me on the path to healing. He showed me how to start a new life.

Clive refused to take credit for guiding me to that point. He said it was my spirit, some intangible force within me, that had allowed me to rise above the ashes of my past. I believe that his faith in me, his intuitive belief in natural healing, his unstinting support of my decisions, gave me the tools I needed to rebuild an interrupted life.

Because so many people were genuinely concerned about my welfare, I agreed that I would first go to Cape Town on a visit and stay with friends. Although I felt more in control of my life than at any point since the murders, I admit that I was still somewhat fragile. I had mined the issues of guilt and regret, traipsed up and down the avenue of 'what-ifs', visited every possible scenario in search of answers. I was acutely aware that I was still in the clutches of post-traumatic stress disorder, and that some symptoms – panic attacks, moments

Homeward bound

of unreasonable fear, anger and sadness – would probably recur throughout my life. Clive and I had talked at length about how some of my former friends would probably not feature in my 'new' life and that I would need to forge new bonds in time. I had no expectation of Cape Town meaning the same to me as it had before. I knew how important it would be to avoid undue stress and continue taking baby steps to build my self-confidence and shore up my newfound independence.

Shaun had been right when he'd said: 'Only Debbie knows what Debbie needs.' My primary identity had shifted to that of survivor, and I had learned not to feel guilty about that. I would have to steel myself to face the full horror yet again, revisit my previous life as often as it took to reach some sense of closure. I could not run from reality forever, or remain caught up in the past indefinitely.

It was time to retrieve the key to my future from the ruins of my past, and the only place I could do that was Cape Town.

14

A new beginning

My visit to Cape Town in March 2003 was for only a week, but in that time I found a townhouse and signed a six-month lease. I consulted no one before signing on the dotted line, promising myself that I would do everything possible to protect my independence. I had been wholly dependent on Tony and, for the last year, on my parents. Now I wanted to live by and for myself.

Previously, dependency had felt warm and somehow comforting. Now it frightened me and felt quite wrong. I not only wanted to stand on my own two feet and make my own decisions, I needed to do so, for the sake of my sanity.

Telling my parents that I'd found somewhere to live and that I fully intended going back to Cape Town as soon as possible was tricky. They worried that it was too soon, that I'd made a rash decision, but in the end they found the courage to let me go.

My brother Bruce went with me. It was May, almost exactly a year since I had boarded that aircraft for Durban in floods of tears. We drove directly to Karen and Michael's house, a surge of energy and excitement coursing through my veins as I recognised the familiar streets and buildings.

Michael's house, on the other hand, felt totally different. So much had changed since I had last been there. Instead of four adults with five children between them, there were now only two of each.

Bruce stayed for four days, going with me from store to store to buy a washing machine, dishwasher and other appliances I would need. Items from the Marina da Gama house were taken out of storage and, in no time at all, my little townhouse was ready for occupation. When the time came for Bruce to leave, Michael took him to the airport. I stood at the gate of my new home, waving until they turned the corner.

It was when I went inside, locking the front door behind me, that I realised I was completely alone for the first time in more than a year. Feeling rather apprehensive and not knowing what to do with myself, I wandered aimlessly from room to room. Then Isobel telephoned.

'Are you okay?' she asked. 'Why don't you come over, sleep here tonight? It might make it easier to get this first night behind you.'

For a moment, I was tempted. I felt some of the tension drain from my muscles at the thought of how safe I would feel at Isobel's house, but something told me it was now or never. I had to try to get through at least one night on my own. In the morning I might want to reconsider my decision to go it alone, but if I left now, I might never again find the courage to become independent.

Scared and wracked with doubt, I tried convincing myself that I was fine. I thought about making something to eat, but I wasn't quite ready to face a solitary pot bubbling on the stove. As a wave of self-pity washed over me, I went to sit in the

A new beginning

living room and paged through a magazine. It was almost nine o'clock, so I decided to go to bed.

I went upstairs and lay down among the children's teddy bears that I had scattered on my bed. Framed, enlarged photographs of Kevin, Katelyn and Craig stared back at me in the semi-darkness. The emptiness in the room was almost palpable. I closed my eyes, then opened them almost immediately. I'd suddenly remembered that I could take a bath! I jumped up and started running the water. Then I remembered something else. I had a radio! I took it with me to the bathroom, the volume turned up high to banish the silence.

Back in bed, I flipped through another magazine and left the radio on. I was hungry, but I didn't fancy going downstairs again, so after a while I turned off the music and the light and closed my eyes. 'You are safe,' I told myself. 'No one can get to you.'

I slept through the night but, as had become usual, awoke in tears and with a sense of dread. I had chosen to live alone, but I had no job and seemed no closer to accepting that my children were gone forever. I spent the next few days crying and reviewing my situation. Finally, I forced myself to listen to the voice in my head that kept urging me to do something, however small a step it was.

First I telephoned a man called Raymond, and we arranged that he would come to my house the following evening. Then I called Shaun and made a hair appointment.

In the chaotic aftermath of events in January 2002, my parents had taken the advice of a friend and placed our dogs, Hazel and Henry, in the care of Raymond and his wife, Lorraine. They loved animals and were happy to have them.

One of my early concerns, after regaining consciousness, had been the whereabouts of the dogs. My father had assured me that they were in good hands and, once I got to Amanzimtoti, I telephoned Raymond periodically to find out how they were. He and Lorraine were absolute angels. Not only did they give both dogs a loving home, they also told me that if I were ever in a position to have them live with me again, they would understand.

There was no way I would be able to manage two dogs, but I missed them dreadfully. Finally, Raymond, Lorraine and I decided that Hazel would 'come home' to me, while Henry would remain with them.

Now that day had come, and I waited anxiously at the gate until Raymond's car appeared and drew up in front of my house. I caught sight of Hazel on the back seat and felt a little faint. I had longed for a reunion with the dog that had been so close to my children, but I had no idea how she would react. Would she still know me? Would it be hard for her to leave Raymond and Lorraine? How sad would they be to lose her? What would be best for both the dog and me?

Raymond opened the car door and Hazel jumped out and ran towards me. I put out my hand and touched her. She let me stroke and fondle her for a short while, then jogged back to Raymond's side. He walked into the house with her, stayed for a few minutes and left. It was clear that parting with Hazel was not easy for him, and I am most grateful to her 'foster owners' for looking after and loving Hazel enough to let me have her back. They are generous and caring people – pure angels, and Henry lives like a king!

A new beginning

Raymond had told me that when Hazel first came to them, and for a long time afterwards, she was visibly and seriously traumatised. She would flop down on her tummy, put her front paws together, drop her head onto them and simply cry. She was so terrified of noise that, for months, Raymond and Lorraine had to watch television with the sound turned down. Any loud noise would send Hazel crawling into a dark corner and refusing to come when called.

As she and I stared at one another in the living room that evening, I wondered if she would be able to make yet another major adjustment. I stroked her gently and gave her something to eat. When I went to the bathroom, she followed me and lay on the floor, but when I went back downstairs to make a cup of tea, I noticed she was not with me. I went to my bedroom and there she was, fast asleep on the bed, surrounded by the children's teddy bears. She seemed content, lifting her head briefly when I climbed into bed, then resting it again while I patted her. 'We are going to be all right,' I told her gently.

Shaun had squeezed me into his routinely hectic schedule, and as I walked into the salon, he stormed towards me. We had not seen one another for more than a year and we hugged for at least five minutes. During our phone chats, he had made me promise that I would not let anyone in Durban cut my hair. I had gone to a hairdresser in Amanzimtoti three times, and on the last visit she had indeed suggested that it was time for a cut. 'Maybe next time,' I'd said, Shaun's face uppermost in my mind. I had not returned to that salon.

Now, as Shaun cut and highlighted my 'new' hair for the first time, it was wonderful to be able to talk to someone I trusted and felt so comfortable with. By the time I left, not only had my flagging spirits been lifted, but my hair looked damn good too!

As had happened so many times after 16 January 2002, good friends and total strangers conspired to set me back on my feet. Unbeknown to me, Shaun had mentioned to another client, after I left the salon, that I was looking for a job. She called her husband there and then, and later in the day I was telephoned by a man who said he'd got my number from Shaun. He had just started a business and needed a receptionist. Would I be interested?

Would I! I was overwhelmed. I got the job and, more importantly, my self-confidence received a massive boost. It was just six weeks since I had set foot in Cape Town again and already I had a new home, a source of income and a furry four-legged companion.

Finding a job had been one of the biggest hurdles I knew I'd have to face. The trust fund set up after the murders had been one of my greatest blessings, but most of it had been used to cover my medical and rehabilitation expenses. There had been three relatively small insurance policies that paid out after Tony died, and I had R20 000 put away following the sale of equipment at the Redham House tuck shop. I knew that Tony had opened bank accounts for each of our children, but could not remember at which branches, and, of course, he had burned all our financial documents.

I'd spent hours telephoning the banks in search of those accounts. Each time, I had to explain why I had no records or references, and none of my calls produced results. A few weeks later, I went to collect the backlog of mail that had gone to our

A new beginning

postbox in Constantia during my absence. There was so much of it that a postal assistant kindly offered to help me sort through the pile. Among the many envelopes, he found one addressed to Master K Adlington. It was from a bank – one that I had telephoned, as a matter of fact. The enclosed letter pointed out that, in the absence of any activity on Kevin's account for quite some time, it had become dormant. Did he wish to keep the account open?

I burst into tears. Obviously I could not expect a financial institution to have taken note via the media of my son's death, but it was an eerie experience to read mail that clearly assumed he was alive. I took the letter to the bank the next day and explained to an assistant why Master Adlington had not responded to their letter. She promptly burst into tears, which of course set me off as well, so there we were, two women sobbing on opposite sides of the counter in a suburban bank.

Eventually, she stopped crying long enough to explain the situation to the manager, who agreed to release the funds and close the account. It was only a small amount, and I never did find the accounts for Katelyn and Craig.

Kevin's tiny cash injection was the last windfall that came my way. There was no other money and plenty of holes that had to be plugged in addition to everyday living expenses. Thanks to my father, I had been able to keep Karen's BMW, but finding a job was crucial if I wanted to stay in Cape Town and be independent. Thanks to Shaun and his thoughtful client, that hurdle had now been cleared.

The night before I started work, I slept badly. I was fretful about getting to the office on time and whether or not I'd be able to handle my new responsibilities. In the morning it was drizzling and I could see that winter was upon us. My route was the same one I had driven hundreds of times while taking Katelyn to school. As I approached the intersection where I would have turned left to go to Springfield Convent, I felt my chest growing tight and had difficulty breathing. The realisation that I no longer had a reason to travel down that road had triggered a full-scale panic attack.

When I was calm enough to continue my journey, I found myself in the right-hand lane, and decided I didn't have the nerve to face the oncoming early morning traffic at such close quarters. I suppose I was distracted, because as I moved my car over to the left, I heard a bang. My rear-view mirror quickly confirmed that I had nudged a vehicle that I hadn't even noticed while switching lanes.

Fortunately, the damage was minimal, but when we exchanged details, the other driver said I would have to talk to her sister, who actually owned the car. I called her later in the day, and as soon as I gave my name, she asked: 'Aren't you the lady from Marina da Gama?' As we spoke, it turned out that she had also lost a child, and the accident that morning was all but forgotten as we shared our feelings and coping mechanisms. My first day at work had started badly, but it ended well enough.

The job itself proved to be stress-free and undemanding, for which I was grateful. Still, I was physically exhausted by the time I got home in the evenings and fell asleep quite early. The important thing was that a full-time job gave me a reason to get out of bed each day and somewhere to go, both major antidotes for depression.

A new beginning

Hazel simply would not stay home alone. The moment she heard the jangle of my keys, she would run to the front door in anticipation and follow me to the car. Every morning on the way to work I dropped her off at a friend's house in Plumstead, and every evening I would fetch her again from her 'doggie day care'. When I went shopping over weekends, Hazel went as well. I'd find a shady parking bay, give her a bowl of water, and pay one of the security guards to keep an eye on my car and its canine occupant.

Life seemed to get a little easier and more purposeful every day, though I was still emotionally fragile and the most insignificant thing could release floods of tears. Weekends were especially hard. To alleviate the loneliness during the long, idle hours, I would head for the nearest shopping mall and my favourite coffee shop, Savannah. Adrian, the owner, had known me for years. He had known my children, too, so he understood why, many times, I broke down at the corner table to which I always gravitated. He sat there with me hour after hour, talking, comforting or in sympathetic silence.

It added to my sense of security to frequent shops that I had come to know while married. Pick 'n Pay in Plumstead was one of these places. I had shopped there for years, dragging the kids behind me, and I continued to buy my monthly groceries there. The manager and staff were absolute gems. They remembered how the children and I would scoot up and down the aisles, filling our trolleys with whatever was needed at home or for the tuck shop, then visit the in-house coffee shop for refreshments before leaving.

The manager, John Coetzee, almost always stopped at

our table for a chat and he always had a friendly word for the children. Both Savannah and Pick 'n Pay had made generous contributions to the trust fund, and the only way I could repay their kindness was by continuing to be a loyal customer.

When I returned to Cape Town and began visiting Pick 'n Pay again, the staff 'adopted' me for very special attention. They would prepare a meal for me each time I shopped, sometimes asking what I felt like and, at other times, surprising me. The food was always good, and for a long time, that would be my main meal on 'shopping day'.

One evening after work, I noticed a little boy at the deli counter with his mother. He was pleading for a sausage. Without thinking, I said, 'Let me get it for him.' The assistant gave the child a sausage and passed me the till slip. As I walked away, I suddenly thought I might have given offence. After all, he wasn't my child and his mother might have had good reason for not buying her son a sausage. A great sadness came over me as I realised how thoughtless and impulsive I had been and I stood there, in the middle of the store, and wept. One of the employees came and helped me to a seat in the coffee shop, insisting that I drink something to calm down. The kindness and consideration of the staff at that store have been truly amazing.

Inevitably, there was no escaping the memories. My family had lived in Cape Town for a long time and it was unavoidable that I would go to places we had visited together, bump into my children's school friends or teachers from time to time, or retrace steps I had formerly taken with Kevin, Katelyn or Craig by my side. Most of the time I could cope, but then

A new beginning

something would happen unexpectedly and I'd realise that no matter how much progress I had made, I was not fully healed and probably never would be.

Anniversaries evoked the worst kind of sadness and longing. As Katelyn's birthday approached in August, I had to step up the daily battle against the gremlins of grief. One evening, as I fell into bed, exhausted, I pulled the children's teddy bears into my arms – a habit I had recently acquired – and was just about to turn out the light when my eye caught a small dark spot on one of the soft toys.

I sat up immediately, turning the teddy bear every which way under the bedside lamp. My spirits sank as I stared at the small but unmistakeable spot on Kevin's bear. It was unquestionably blood – Kevin's blood, spilled that dreadful night. It took weeks for me to get over the shock of that awful reminder.

Exactly six months after returning to Cape Town, I called Pastor John Miller and asked him to perform a small and private service at which I could say my final farewell to my children. I had never felt ready to do it before, but now I needed that closure I'd heard so much about. I still felt that my children were alive, just not with me. Perhaps they were on holiday, or at school. If the normal mind plays tricks on one, the traumatised mind has a repertoire of illusions that would make David Copperfield look like an amateur.

I knew that I needed the finality of a formal service to help me accept that my children were gone forever.

On 18 January 2004, I entered the beautiful little chapel in the Tokai Forest with a small group of friends. John had made all the arrangements, and the three boxes containing my children's ashes were on a table at the front of the church. The ceremony was simple, brief and devastatingly final. Every fibre of my being rebelled against the fact that I would never again know a moment of joy on earth with Kevin, Katelyn and Craig, but I finally accepted that they were gone, in the cruellest possible manner, and would never come home again.

The life I had given to three special human beings had been taken by their father almost exactly two years before, but for me, this was finally the end.

After the service we walked along a little footpath into the forest. As the trees began to tower over our heads and form an umbrella of leaves dotted with silver-blue patches of sky, we left the path and headed down a slight embankment to a flat and shady patch of grass. After obtaining the necessary permission from the authorities, John had planted a simple wooden cross there.

I stood quite still and stared at the cross. This was probably one of the most peaceful spots in the forest that Kevin, Katelyn and Craig had loved so much. Hazel would lead the way as they gambolled and ran with unbridled joy through the beauty provided by nature.

I opened the container holding Kevin's ashes and let them be swept up by the light breeze before coming to rest around the cross, turning the grass a soft grey. I took Katelyn's ashes next, kissed and opened the wooden box and let the contents drift softly on the wind before they, too, fell to the grass. Craig's were the last, and as my youngest son's ashes spilled onto the grass to mingle with those of his brother and sister, I felt a sickening sadness.

A new beginning

We sat there for a while. I took in the finality of it all. I promised to return often to be with them. I stroked my hand ever so gently over the grass, watching the ash colour my fingers slightly. Then, suddenly, the wind changed and only the cross remained. The last physical matter that had made up my beloved and beautiful babies was gone, claimed by the breeze and blown away forever.

15

Alone no more

To be told in February 2005 that I was pregnant made me indescribably happy. Relief that the IVF procedure had been successful, first time round, was coupled with immense joy at the prospect of being a mother again.

Midway through my pregnancy, the sight on a computer screen of my baby gently moving, touching her face, turning slightly in my womb, was the most powerful testimony to my survival. I think it was at that moment in my gynaecologist's rooms that I was able to acknowledge fully and for the first time that I still had a lot of life to live. Yes, I would always bear the scars. My left hand was pretty much incapacitated, the fingers stiff and movement minimal, despite endless exercises. My left arm was weak and my left leg dragged slightly when I walked. But I had taken a giant leap into the future and found that I could hope and dream again.

As the gynaecologist measured my baby's waist, legs, abdominal circumference, heart rate and facial features, my thoughts turned to Tony. The last time I had seen a baby in my womb, he had been with me. Finally able to picture his face without feeling extreme anger, I remembered how he had smiled and pointed out Craig's tiny nose and hands.

It had taken more than three years to reach a point where I could start feeling sorry for Tony. How sad that he had given up on life and rejected the love he could have had from his children and me in years to come. How fearful and desperate he must have been. How terrible it must have been for him to end his life knowing that his children had died by their father's hands. Yes, I could forgive him, but I could not excuse or understand his actions. I never will.

As Kylie-Ann's birth drew closer, I became increasingly uncomfortable, both physically and emotionally. I wish I could say that I was brave throughout, but I wasn't. I often wondered if everything would be all right and became stressed about the smallest things.

On 12 November 2005, my friend Liz picked me up at home and drove me to the Constantiaberg Medi-Clinic. Her husband Monty was to deliver my baby. Their eldest child, Nicholas, had been a friend of Kevin's. Liz is a nurse, and I felt confident that between her, Monty and Isobel, I would be in good hands during my self-induced ordeal.

Delivery rooms had made great strides since Craig's birth thirteen years earlier. The super-efficient staff monitored the baby and me closely as my labour progressed and, around 3 p.m., with the contractions increasing in both frequency and intensity, Monty decided that a Caesarean delivery was called for. The baby was quite big and he thought natural birth could be a problem.

I was wheeled to the theatre with Isobel and Liz in tow, Liz acting as my breathing coach. Thanks to an epidural, I was awake when Monty put his hands into my uterus and lifted the baby out. He turned her to face me, and I saw her for a few seconds before she was whisked away to be examined by the paediatrician. Then she was wrapped in a soft blanket and brought to me to hold for the first time.

At 3.6 kilograms, Kylie-Anne was the biggest of all my children, and she was beautiful. I wept for joy as I cradled her in my arms. No matter what the future held, whatever we might have to face, we would do it together and with abundant love.

As with the birth of all my children, my parents came to stay with me for several weeks after Kylie-Ann was born. The day after they left to travel home to Amanzimtoti was a very special one, even in what had been an eventful year. In May, I had taken full control of my finances again for the first time since 2002. I'd managed to put down a deposit on my townhouse and buy a small home industry outlet at the Blue Route Mall in Tokai that offered me a comfortable enough income.

Tomorrow, Kylie-Ann and I would go back to work, but today, we had somewhere else to go.

My mom had bathed Kylie-Ann for the first weeks of her life. Now I knelt beside the bath and ran a few centimetres of water into the tub. I grabbed my left hand with my right and pushed my left arm to the middle of the bath, folding my inert fingers into a fist. With my strong right arm, I lifted my naked baby out of her stroller and gently laid her in the water, her head resting on my clenched left hand. Crooning soft words of reassurance, I soaped her little body.

'There you are. See, it doesn't matter that Mommy's hand doesn't work so well. We'll always find a way. You love your bath, don't you?'

Later, holding Kylie-Ann in my arms, I followed the familiar path from the chapel in the Tokai Forest to the wooden cross planted in honour of her brothers and sister. I walked slowly and deliberately, taking extra care not to slip or fall as I made my way around the trees and down the little slope.

Hazel had already reached the cross. She liked to get there first, running ahead, sniffing the forest floor, making sure the path was safe. I am always relieved to see that the cross is still there, undamaged.

It was a glorious early December morning. The wind rustled through the trees as I set Kylie-Ann down in her carrycot and sat down next to her on the patch of wild grass. She opened her eyes, gazing up at the green leaves overhead. I wondered if she could see that far, and rocked her gently as she turned her face towards me. Katelyn had also loved being rocked, and Kevin had quickly learned how to set her carrycot in motion.

Sometimes, I had to warn you not to be too enthusiastic, didn't I, Kevin? It's so nice that we can be here together, the four of us. Mommy is happy to have Kylie-Ann, and I know you love her too. Isn't she pretty? She reminds Mommy of Craig. Remember that chubby little body that I loved to cuddle? Karen must be so jealous of my beautiful baby girl. Look, here comes Hazel, panting from running around in the forest. She misses the three of you. See how she looks at Kylie-Ann, wanting to lick her tiny hands. Now she's lying down beside me, watching over us. Hazel seems content, at peace again. That's how Mommy's feeling, too. You will always be part of my life, but I'm not scared any more. Rest in peace, my darlings. We'll come to visit often, I promise, and you will be with me and Kylie-Ann always.

Alone no more

Recently, I read a book[*] about dealing with life after loss. It encapsulated perfectly what I had experienced, and one passage in particular summed up my journey since January 2002:

> If we are alive, we cannot escape loss. Loss is part of real life. There is a story of a woman who lost her only child and was bereft, inconsolable and alone.
>
> She went to Buddha to ask his help in healing her wounded spirit. If he couldn't, she would follow her child to the grave and forgo her destiny. Karma be damned. She would not, could not continue to live this way.
>
> The Buddha agreed to help but told the mother she must first bring him back a mustard seed from a house that had never known sorrow. And so the woman set out to find one.
>
> Her search took her a long time. She went from house to house all over the world but there was not one that had never entertained grief as a guest. However, because every house knew what her pain felt like, they wanted to give her a gift to help ease her anguish. It could not make it go away, but it might help.
>
> When the woman returned home she opened her heart and showed the Buddha what she had been given: acceptance, understanding, gratitude, courage, compassion, hope, truth, empathy, remembrance, strength, tenderness, wisdom and love.
>
> 'These gifts were given to help me,' she told him.
>
> 'Ah, they were? And how do you feel now?' he asked the woman.

---

[*] *Something More – Excavating Your Authentic Self* by Sarah Ban Breathnach, Bantam Books, London, 1998, pp 226–7.

'Different. Heavier. Each gift comforts me in its own way, but there were so many, I had to enlarge my heart to carry them all and they make me feel sated. What is this strange full feeling?'

'Sorrow.'

'You mean I'm like the others now?'

'Yes,' said the Buddha softly. 'You are no longer alone.'

Reflections

Writing *Mom, Interrupted* inevitably led to reflection on the phenomenon of family murders in South Africa. Whenever they occur, the same questions are asked: Could the tragedy have been avoided? Were there signs that this unspeakable act was about to happen? What could have been done, and by whom, to prevent it?

The Adlington case differs from most family murders in that a key family member – the wife and mother – survived. Usually, answers and explanations have to be sought in the accounts and perceptions of relatives, friends, neighbours and colleagues who, at best, can offer only partial or peripheral insights. Debbie is among a small group of people who have lived to tell the tale of a family's violent end at the hands of one of its own. As such, no one might seem better qualified to answer the searing questions that *must* be posed if professionals and potential victims alike are to understand why some individuals seek solutions to family problems in death rather than divorce or discourse.

In asking what lessons are to be learned from Debbie's story, however, it should be borne in mind that this is not an empirical study. Certainly, there is valuable information to be gleaned and many assumptions will doubtless be drawn, but Debbie's story is essentially a personal and intimate one, coloured by her views and emotions.

Subjective though it is, Debbie's description of her family dynamics and relationships bears a striking similarity to available research on family murder. Every family murder is unique, but there are certain common denominators and indicators that may act as an early warning system, provided they are correctly interpreted. The Adlington case has a number of those hallmarks.

Family murder came under the spotlight in the 1980s, when the media began speculating that it was a phenomenon found mainly among white, Afrikaans-speaking South Africans. There were strong suggestions that it was somehow born of the political instability and conflict raging at the time.

At the beginning of 1990, a large research project was commissioned by the Human Sciences Research Council (HSRC) under the auspices of the then Department of Health and Development. This national study included academics from various social disciplines who studied eleven cases extensively over an eighteen-month period.

Their findings challenged the assumption that family murder was endemic among white Afrikaners. All population groups are vulnerable to what emerged as a complex phenomenon influenced by a multitude of factors. The variables identified by researchers made it impossible to find 'easy' answers to the underlying causes of family murder. The study accepted that 'each family had its own dynamics and behavioural patterns', but attempted to 'identify common elements and similarities that provide a context for family murder, thus leaving out the idiosyncratic patterns of each family'.[1]

It is important to note this, because the factors and patterns within the Adlington family will not be replicated exactly by any other family. One must therefore guard against the presumption that shared elements automatically signal impending doom.

Professor Maria Marchetti-Mercer, head of the psychology department at the University of Pretoria, was involved in the

---

[1] L Olivier, CP Haasbroek, D Beyers, JT de Jongh van Arkel, MC Marchetti, JL Roos, EM Schurink, WJ Schurick and MJ Visser, *The phenomenon of family murder in South Africa: An exploratory study* (Pretoria: HSRC, 1991).

original HSRC study, and subsequently wrote an article on family murders called 'The phenomenon of family murder in South Africa: Some etiological considerations'.[2] In this study, she explored the causes of family murder and possible intervention strategies.

Both the HSRC and the Marchetti-Mercer study adopted the following definition of family murder: '... the deliberate extermination of the existing system by a member of the family or the intention to exterminate the system'.[3] Marchetti-Mercer emphasised that family murder is a complex phenomenon and argued that the complexity of factors that lead to the actual murders in each case are not easily identifiable or quantifiable. She found that there was usually a long-term history of interactive factors and processes that involved all members of the family. This 'circular process of violence' in which all of the relevant factors interact in a highly idiosyncratic manner provides a context for violence, she argued.[4]

According to Marchetti-Mercer, it might be impossible to identify a single common denominator or pattern for the kind of desperation that can lead to a family murder, as each perpetrator and his/her experience of the world are highly individual. Nevertheless, research[5] indicates that:

- Family murders occur among all population groups.
- Family murders occur in many countries of the world.
- The phenomenon seems to be on the increase.

---

2   MC Marchetti-Mercer, 'Family murder in post-apartheid South Africa: Some reflections for mental health professionals', *Health SA Gesondheid*, 8 (2), pp 83–91 (2003).

3   Olivier *et al*, HSRC report.

4   Marchetti-Mercer, 'Family murder in post-apartheid South Africa'.

5   Olivier *et al*, HSRC report; Marchetti-Mercer, 'Family murder in post-apartheid South Africa'; JL Roos, D Beyers, MJ Visser, 'Family murder: Psychiatric and psychological causes', *Geneeskunde*, 34 (8), pp 25–30 (1992).

- In the South African context, the high prevalence of violence may be a factor.

While there is no 'typical' family murderer, the multiple and complex elements that may characterise a perpetrator and contribute to creating a climate conducive to family murder include the following:
- Mood disorders and, specifically, depressive disorders.
- Some personality disorders and dependent personality traits.
- Emotional immaturity, impulsiveness, poor problem-solving skills.
- Feelings of hopelessness and despair.
- Ineffective and immature communication skills.
- Emotional neglect between partners.
- Superficial emotional involvement between partners.
- Dominance by one partner.
- An overdeveloped sense of ultimate responsibility for the family.
- A lack of emotional and psychological support and isolation from the extended family or community.
- Increased stress levels prior to the event.
- A stigma related to psychological and psychiatric trauma that might prevent the family or perpetrator from seeking assistance.
- Relatively easy access to firearms.

Research has shown that the family murderer almost always wears a mask of normality. To outsiders in particular, Tony Adlington was the picture of a devoted family man and good provider. In the words of his business associate, Cape Town real estate agent Bill Rawson: 'Tony was a good and kind man, intelligent, a hard worker and very considerate towards his staff.'

Reflections

Rawson may have been the last person to speak to Tony, just hours before he struck down his wife and children. Yet, even then, there was no hint of what he had in mind.

'I'd noticed that he was taking strain in the weeks before the incident. The franchise was not going as well as he had hoped. We spoke on the phone the night before he died and I specifically asked Tony if something was bothering him, if I could help in any way. He said he was having some financial problems, and I assured him that whatever the difficulty, we could sort it out.

'That was it. Afterwards, it became clear that he really was cash-strapped, but, even so, the problem was not insurmountable. It is the saddest, saddest thing that, in his mind, the only thing that made sense was to destroy his family,' says Rawson.

As far as Rawson was concerned, Tony 'cared deeply for Debbie and loved the children very much'. The man he knew was 'not a monster' – yet there is evidence that he began preparing to kill his family at least six weeks before he acted. Both the axe and the petrol he used were bought at the beginning of December. All through the festive season, even while celebrating Craig's birthday and later Kevin's, his behaviour aroused no suspicion.

No one will ever know what triggered his decision to execute his plan on that specific night. There was no argument or confrontation, no imminent threat to Tony's status as head of the family. Might he thus fit best into the category of killers identified by researchers as acting from a distorted basis of love, believing they are freeing their families from burdens they themselves can no longer bear?

The HSRC study found that family murder was directly related to interaction and relationships within the family, rather than in alternative settings such as the workplace or social circle. The many hours and wide range of activities that family members share, the demands they make on one another, their ages and the fact that some members (such as children) cannot escape the membership can all be contributing factors.[6]

The fact that one family member might assume the right to direct and influence the behaviour of other members can play an important role in laying a path for violent and destructive behaviour. It is the intense emotional involvement and bond between family members that often cause or make the violence possible.[7]

There is no doubt that Tony had loved his wife and children. Despite many difficulties, he never raised the prospect of divorce. He was emotionally attached to the children and had an obvious desire to please and make them happy. The family was close-knit; they spent the bulk of their free time together and depended heavily on one another. Tony had few friends and chose not to share deep issues with them. He not only saw himself as the head of the family and assumed responsibility for their welfare, he also assumed that he had the right to make all decisions on their behalf.

Debbie catalogued a number of major incidents that illustrate Tony's lack of understanding or respect for his wife and children as individual beings, separate from him and with their own distinct right to life. He habitually made unilateral decisions, ruled by emotional force, and seemingly viewed Debbie and the children as mere extensions of himself. They had to do what he said, go when and where he wanted, and follow him without question – to Johannesburg, to Cape Town, to an abortion and, ultimately, to death.

According to family counsellor Duke Mothiba, 'One ongoing problem can be identified at each family murder. Often it comprises a range of problems resulting from difficult and trying work

---

[6] RJ Gelles and MA Strauss, 'Determinants of violence in the family: Towards a theoretical integration' in WB Burr, R Hill, Fl Nye and IL Reiss (eds.), *Contemporary theories about the family* (New York: Free Press, 1979), pp 549–81.

[7] PC Kratcoski, 'Families who kill'. *Marriage and family review*, 12 (1–2), pp 47–70 (1988).

circumstances, an unhappy marriage or financial crisis. Often there are many clear warning signs of a threatening suicide or family murder. Unfortunately, many people refuse to seek assistance because they are of the opinion that something as shameful and horrible as a family murder would not happen within their boundaries. The media and many institutions also apply pressure to create the perfect family. However, no family is perfect, and parents should realise that it is not a shame to have a so-called dysfunctional family.'[8]

Marchetti-Mercer argues that 'there still exists a very strong stigma around psychological and psychiatric help. Medical aid contributions towards psychological services are very limited and most people are unable to afford psychotherapy.'[9]

Family murderers are often jealous, depressed, in debt, emotionally insecure, feel hopeless, desperate, anxious, angry, intensely frustrated, and struggle to socialise and assert themselves.

From what is known, Tony Adlington displayed several of these characteristics. He frequently took an instant dislike to new people that he met, refused to attend his children's school functions, even though this usually meant disappointing them at the last minute, and needed to be in control at all times. His public persona was that of a financially successful man, well on the way to achieving his aim of being a millionaire by the age of fifty. In private, however, he became increasingly abusive — albeit verbally — towards his wife, and evidently cared little that his children were exposed to this behaviour.

Because the marital subsystem is the heart of any family's functionality, it affects every member of the group. The way in

---

[8] Mrs Duke Mothiba (national director of the Family and Marriage Association of South Africa, FAMSA) in 'Family murders — the selfish ending of loved one's lives', *Servamus* (May 2005).

[9] Marchetti-Mercer, 'Family murder in post-apartheid South Africa'.

which parents communicate with one another, the depth of their emotional commitment and how they define their roles determine whether or not theirs is a 'happy' family. Communication between couples involved in family murders was generally found to have been ineffective and superficial.[10] Messages were often relayed indirectly, thereby paving the way for misunderstanding and conflict. Emotional neglect was frequently present. 'It seemed as if the control for power, as well as the conflict and tension alternating between apathy and emotional distance, characterised the interaction between the murderer and spouse. However, in the end the murderer gained ultimate control by dominating through murder.'[11]

By Debbie's own admission, she and Tony failed to discuss their problems or share their emotions. Divorce might not have been a serious consideration, but Debbie was often unhappy. Tony might have felt the same, yet neither was willing to raise issues that might cause a ripple in their established, day-to-day routine. From time to time, at least, they lived past one another, even though they were under the same roof.

Debbie's dream of a stable and successful marriage might well have masked the reality that this was a family that stayed together despite many difficulties. Tony's ongoing search for financial betterment, even when this meant moving halfway across the country, caused an undercurrent of resentment from a relatively early stage of their marriage. In the end, perhaps he simply could not face the fact that fortune had eluded him and that he was mere days away from being exposed as a failure, especially in his children's eyes.

According to Marchetti-Mercer, 'As far as the perpetrators

---

10 *Ibid.*

11 D Beyers, M Visser and MC Marchetti, 'The family context: Processes and interaction in family murder', *Geneeskunde*, 34 (9), pp 3–7 (1992).

Reflections

of family murders are concerned, the reality seems to have been created in their lives that there is neither end, nor solution to their desperation and that no help to their problem is available.'[12]

More often than not, she cautions, 'overly simplistic explanations are sought to explain this type of violence. These fail to address the complex phenomenon of a father or mother who decides to kill his/her own family as well as taking his/her life. These types of explanations often also take away the responsibility from society and its mental health professionals. A society needs to be created in which death and violence are not the only realities available to people. In this sense we have a social responsibility as mental health professionals to create structures and support systems which allow people to explore other alternatives when faced with what they perceive to be desperate situations.

'In a country wrought with economic problems and also facing a pandemic of HIV/AIDS, money for mental health services seems very limited. However, unless a society can be created where mental health issues are regarded as [being as] important as other economic, social and political issues, desperate people with psychological problems for which they see no solution will still seek violent solutions.

'Our responsibility as mental health professionals is to move beyond the realm of academia or private practice. We have a responsibility to create a public awareness and a social context where psychological problems are approached in a humane and empathic manner.'[13]

As with the Adlingtons, the alternative is irreversible and utterly devastating. In the absence of greater awareness, more research, destigmatisation of psychological and emotional disorders, and

---

12 Olivier *et al*, HSRC report.
13 Marchetti-Mercer, 'Family murder in post-apartheid South Africa'.

availability of preventive measures, our society will continue to be haunted by the question 'why?' each time another family suffers the same fate.

AUTHOR'S NOTE: Special thanks to Professor Maria Marchetti-Mercer, whose research greatly assisted in gaining a better insight into the phenomenon of family murder.

Do you have any comments, suggestions or feedback about this book or any other Zebra Press titles? Contact us at **talkback@zebrapress.co.za**